LOVE
BASICSfor
CATHOLICS

"As Pope St. John Paul II's Theology of the Body unveiled the 'spousal meaning of the body,' Bergsma offers us a masterclass on what could be called the 'spousal meaning of the Bible.' Through his trademark teaching style, simplicity, and humor, you will see love, marriage, and family in thrilling clarity as both human and divine, historical and eternal, personal and universal. We'll call this required reading for all our couples!"

Damon and Melanie Owens
Cofounders of *Joyful Ever After*

"*Love Basics for Catholics* is John Bergsma at his very best! Witty, engaging, inspiring, every chapter takes the reader deeper and deeper into the mind and heart of God through his sacred Word. This book proves, once again, that Bergsma is not only a keen biblical mind but also a masterful teacher, taking the most profound and deepest scriptural truths and making them understandable and digestible for any age. This little gem is a must read for all Catholics!"

Mark Hart
Coauthor of *Our Not-Quite-Holy Family*

"Pope emeritus Benedict XVI wrote that love is not a command but a response. In *Love Basics for Catholics*, John Bergsma uses the greatest romances in scripture to help us respond to love by highlighting the greatest love of all: the covenant between God and man. Every reader will enjoy this deep dive into the Bible's dynamic duos. Lighthearted and profound, this book is a must read."

Deacon Jason and Rachel Bulman
Contributors to Word on Fire Catholic Ministries

"In this popular biblical survey of salvation history, John Bergsma shows how marital love is at the heart of God's plan in both the Old and New Testaments. This small book is deceptively simple. It is clear yet deep, practical yet profound. Indeed, only someone who is both a great scholar and a master teacher could've written it. And the line drawings make the lessons more memorable and teachable—for all ages! Highly recommended."

Scott Hahn
Catholic theologian

LOVE
BASICS for
CATHOLICS

Illustrating God's Love for Us
throughout the Bible

JOHN BERGSMA

Ave Maria Press AVE Notre Dame, Indiana

Nihil Obstat: Reverend Monsignor Michael Heintz, PhD
                     Censor librorum
Imprimatur: Most Reverend Kevin C. Rhoades
                     Bishop of Fort Wayne–South Bend
                     November 25, 2022

Founded in 1865, Ave Maria Press is a ministry of the United States Province of Holy Cross.

www.avemariapress.com

Paperback: ISBN-13 978-1-64680-196-1

E-book: ISBN-13 978-1-64680-197-8

Cover and text design by Andy Wagoner.

Illustrations rendered by Andy Wagoner.

Printed and bound in the United States of America.

Library of Congress Cataloging-in-Publication Data is available.

Contents

Introduction: Who Wrote the Book of Love? 1

One Adam and Eve 7

Two Noah and His Wife 19

Three Abraham and Sarah 29

Four God and Israel at Sinai 43

Five Boaz and Ruth 53

Six Solomon and His Bride: The Song of Songs 65

Seven God and Israel in the Prophets 81

Eight Jesus the Bridegroom: The Gospel of John 91

Nine Christ and the Church: Paul's Letter to
the Ephesians.. 105

Ten The Lamb and the New Jerusalem: The Book
of Revelation 123

Eleven What Can We Learn? 133

Notes 147

Introduction

Who Wrote the Book of Love?

In 1958, a vocal band called the Monotones—made up of six friends from a church choir in Newark—released a song that shot to the top of the charts, titled "Book of Love." If you've never heard it, stop now and look it up on YouTube. It's a very catchy tune—fun to sing and fun to dance to. But sadly for the Monotones, it was a one-hit wonder. None of their other songs ever climbed the charts, and they disbanded in 1962. Yet even decades later when I was growing up, you could still hear their iconic song every now and again on the radio.

And for good reason. The song asks a profound question: Who wrote the Book of Love? The Monotones were on the right track when they guessed, "Was it someone from above?" In the following pages, we'll see that God is the one who wrote the Book of Love, and we usually call it the Bible.

That may sound surprising. Most people probably do not think of the Bible as a book about love, much less *the* Book of Love. They would probably say it was a book of law, history, or old myths, but not *love*. But the Bible is primarily about love from beginning to end, from Genesis to Revelation. The Bible story begins with the wedding of the first man and woman in a garden called Eden, and it ends with the wedding of someone called "the Lamb" and his bride in a heavenly city called Jerusalem. And right in the middle of the Bible is a strange book called the Song of Songs that is nothing but a collection of romantic poetry, in which King Solomon romances his newlywed "princess bride." So at the beginning, middle, and end of the Bible we have weddings.

The themes of love and marriage fill the in-between material, too. Most of the first book of the Bible, Genesis, is concerned with the marriages of Abraham, Isaac, and Jacob, the ancestors of the people of Israel. The second book of the Bible, Exodus, tells how the Israelites left Egypt and went out to Mt. Sinai in the desert, where they were "wedded" to God and became his people. The people of Israel would go on to leave the desert and enter the land God promised them, and in time, God gave them a king named David, who acted in God's place like a husband for the entire people. David's descendants also reigned and were supposed to be royal bridegrooms for Israel. But most of them weren't good husbands, so to speak, so the great prophets predicted that sometime in the future, God himself would visit his people and become their perfect bridegroom once again.

These prophecies were fulfilled centuries later, when Jesus of Nazareth appeared and announced to Israel that God's kingdom had arrived. Jesus used parables to describe this kingdom as a wedding, saying that "the kingdom of heaven may be compared to a king who gave a marriage feast for his son" (Mt 22:1) and that "the kingdom of heaven shall be compared to ten maidens who took their lamps and went to meet the bridegroom" (Mt 25:1). In parables like these, it's clear that the bridegroom is Jesus himself. No one understood this better than Jesus's close friend and disciple John, who later wrote the biography of Jesus (the Gospel of John) that describes him as a bridegroom whose "wedding" was actually his death on a cross! But who is his bride? A later follower of Jesus, the apostle Paul, insisted that those who followed Jesus, the Church, were his bride (see Ephesians 5). And John again, writing the last book of the Bible, had a vision of the Church-as-bride enjoying heaven as an eternal wedding celebration with "the Lamb," Jesus her bridegroom (Rv 20–22). So, from beginning to end, the Bible is a book of love—and not just any love, but that special love between a man and a woman that becomes the unbreakable bond we call marriage.

If this brief, love-focused overview of the Bible moved a little quickly for you, don't worry. That's the purpose of the rest of this book: to move more slowly through each stage of the "romance" between God and his people. These stages, added together, make up the story of the Bible.

A little background on some Bible terms would be helpful before we get started. One word that we'll have to understand is *covenant*. The word "covenant" appears frequently in the Bible. We also hear it used at every Mass, where the Eucharist is called the "new and eternal covenant." But just what *is* a covenant? Some people think it's another word for "contract," "law," or "duty." But actually, a covenant is a family bond made by swearing an oath. Some scholars call it "the extension of kinship by oath." How do you bring someone into your family if they aren't already related to you? You make a covenant with them by swearing an oath.

In the ancient world, and even in many places today, there were two primary forms of covenant: marriage and adoption. That is why the Bible often describes God as either the *father* or the *husband* of his people. At Mt. Sinai, with Moses officiating, God made a solemn covenant with the people of Israel. The Israelites sometimes viewed that covenant as a marriage with God as husband. Other times, they saw it as an adoption with God as Father. Both perspectives are true.

Another term we have to define is *marriage*. We use this word a lot and think we know what it means, but do we really? The Bible shows us that God intended a marriage to be a complete union of one man and one woman for life, for the purpose of raising a family. Even in the pages of the Bible, we read about people not respecting this intention and taking more than one spouse, divorcing a spouse, or misusing marriage in some other way. People continue to do so today, and even the word "marriage" now gets used to describe many different kinds of relationships between people. But it's important to know that, in God's eyes, this is an unbreakable covenant between one man and one woman as long as they both shall live.

And finally, we should talk about what we mean by *love*. People use this word to describe many different kinds of attraction or affection. We say things like, "I love my friends!" or "I love my mom!" or "I love pizza!" In each case, the kind of "love" we are talking about is quite different, even if the word is the same. That can lead to confusion. Hopefully, the love you feel for your mom is a very different kind of emotion than the "love" you have for pizza or your favorite sports team!

Other languages have more than one word for love. The New Testament was written in Greek, which has at least three words for love:

- *eros* (AY-ross), romantic and/or physical attraction;
- *philos* (FEE-loss), friendly or brotherly love; and
- *agapē* (AH-gah-pay), selfless love.

The Old Testament was written in Hebrew. It has a general word for love, *ahavah* (ah-hah-vah), which is a lot like our English word. But Hebrew also has a very special word for love that we don't have in English: *hesed* (HEH-sed).

The word *hesed* refers to the kind of love that family members should have for one another. It includes affection, but its most important feature is *faithfulness*—always keeping one's commitments, never walking away, always being there for the other person, even when it hurts. In the New Testament, the Hebrew word *hesed* was translated into Greek as either "mercy" (*eleos*) or "love" (*agapē*). We will talk a lot about *hesed* in this book because it's the deepest form of love and the form that God describes as his own love.

The Monotones actually describe *hesed* in their song "Book of Love." In their imaginary Book of Love, chapter one says to "love her with all your heart," and chapter two insists "you're never gonna part"—that is what the Bible calls *hesed*, the love that spouses have for one another.

Those are enough definitions! It's time to jump into the Bible as the Book of Love. Starting with Adam and Eve, we are going to look at some of the great romances in the Bible—such as Abraham and Sarah, or Boaz and Ruth—and see that they are images of the one great romance of God and his people. Along the way, we will learn about the importance of marriage in God's plan for our salvation, pick up some tips on how Christians should love and marry, and even discover some things about what heaven will be like. So, let's get started!

One
Adam and Eve

According to the Bible, God created the world for marriage. I know that sounds bold, but hang with me and I'll show you what I mean.

We are all familiar with the story of the six days of creation. In the beginning, when God first called the world into existence, it was "without form and void" (Gn 1:2). In three days, God formed the world, establishing time on the first day, space on the second, and a livable habitat on the third. Then he filled the world he had formed. He filled time with the sun, moon, and stars. He filled the great spaces with birds and fish. Finally, he filled the habitat with animals and man. I've shown in my book *Bible Basics for Catholics* that God was building creation as a great temple like the one shown here, with humanity—the man and woman—as royal priests to rule it.

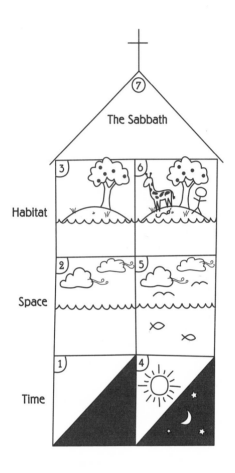

The Hebrew word for "mankind" or "humanity" is *adam*, which is also the personal name of the first man, Adam. When we get to the creation of *adam*, the Bible says something curious about God. Up to this point, God has just been speaking things into existence. He says "Let there be," things appear, and then he sees that they are good. But with man, God says: "Let *us* make man in *our* image, after our likeness; and let them have dominion over the fish of the sea, and over the birds of the air, and over the cattle, and over all the earth" (Gn 1:26, emphasis added).

What does God mean, "Let *us* make man in *our* image"? Before this, God has just been a single person, but now it sounds like there are more than one of him. So it seems that God is both one and more than one. Funny thing, the same turns out to be true of the man that God makes in his image: "So God created man in his own image, in the image of God he created *him*; male and female he created *them*" (Gn 1:27, emphasis added). Like God, man is both "him" and "them," both one and more than one, both singular and plural. This is part of the mystery of being in God's image and likeness.

After God makes *adam*, both *adam*-male and *adam*-female, he is very pleased with them, and gives them a blessing and command: "Be fruitful and multiply, and fill the earth and subdue it" (Gn 1:28). Now, in order to carry out most of this command—the "be fruitful," "multiply," and "fill" parts—the two forms of *adam* are going to have to get together. They are going to have to unite in marriage. So we see that marriage is central to God's intention for humanity. Human beings cannot do what God commanded them to do unless they join in marriage.

The second chapter of Genesis expands on this theme. Beginning at Genesis 2:4, we get a more detailed account of how *adam* came to be. God molded his body from the dust of the earth, breathed into his nostrils the "breath of life," and placed him in a garden to tend and care for it. So far, so good. In fact, everything has been good so far: the light, the earth, the seas, the plants, the birds and fish . . . all "very good" (Gn 1:31). But now, for the first time,

something in creation is "not good": "It is not good that
the man should be alone," God says. "I will make him a
helper fit for him" (Gn 2:18, RSV).

The Hebrew words for "helper fit for him" deserve
attention. The word for "helper," or simply "help," is *ezer*
(AY-zer). It is a common word in the Bible, but one that
almost always refers to help sent by God or by a king,
never to the help that servants or workers provide. Also,
the word translated "fit for him" is *k'negdô* (kuh-NEG-
doe), a rare term meaning literally "like and facing him,"
the way a pair of matching bookends are similar but face
each other. We could also translate it as "complementary"
or "corresponding to him."

So God brings all the animals he has made to the man
to see what he will name them. This is a big deal, since
God has done all the naming up to this point. Now God is
letting Adam do something Godlike: give a name to something. Adam names all the animals, but none of them are
a "helper fit for him." None of them are "like and facing
him."

Didn't God know none of the animals would work?
Of course he did, but this whole process is for Adam's
benefit. As he looks through all the animals for a suitable
helper, he discovers something about himself and what
he truly needs. Moreover, anticipation builds within him
for the final revealing of the "helper fit for him" because
we appreciate things more when we've had to work and
wait for them.

But Adam will have to do more than just work for
this helper; he will need to sacrifice and give of himself.
God puts Adam into a deep sleep—which for Adam must
have felt like dying—and then performs surgery. He opens

Adam's flesh to remove a rib (Gn 2:21–22). Interestingly, the word for "rib" here (Hebrew *tzēla'* [tsay-LAH]) is never used for a part of the body elsewhere in the Bible but almost always for the "ribs"—that is, the supports or beams—that held up the tabernacle or the Temple. This suggests that Adam's body is also a temple. From the rib, God literally "builds" (Hebrew *banah* [bah-NAH]) a woman (2:22, Douay-Rheims). He builds her because she, too, is a temple. We will see this theme of body-as-temple in many other important places in the Bible.

Now God brings Eve to Adam. Before this, Adam has been hanging around with the apes, tossing bananas and showing off his opposable thumb. But once he sees the woman, Adam pulls himself together. This is what he has been waiting for! To find this one, he had to

- search through an endless lineup of animals,
- fall into deathlike sleep,
- let his body be cut open like a sacrifice, and
- make a permanent gift of himself.

Now she appears. Inspired by her loveliness, Adam becomes a poet! Beautiful lyric verse peels off his tongue:

> This at last is bone of my bones
> and flesh of my flesh;
> she shall be called Woman,
> because she was taken out of Man. (Gn 2:23)

This is the high point of the whole story of creation in Genesis. The appearance of the "helper fit for him" is marked not only by the first lyric poetry in the Bible but also by covenant-making language (see 2 Samuel 5:1–3). A covenant is a family formed by an oath. Adam is not just recognizing that Eve has his rib; no, he is *declaring* her to be his flesh-and-bone in a legal sense. He is taking her as family, as spouse.

When families add members through childbirth, each new member gets a name. Likewise, when families are formed by covenant, the new members often get new names (see Genesis 17:5). This is why a bride often takes her husband's name at a wedding. So it is here. Adam forms a new family with this "helper fit for him" and gives her a new name: "woman." Just as in English, so in Hebrew the words for "man" (*'ish* [eesh]) and "woman" (*'ishah* [eesh-AH]) look and sound similar.

This is the first marriage ever, and it has huge implications for the rest of human history. So much so that the sacred author explains: "Therefore a man leaves his father and his mother and cleaves to his wife, and they become one flesh" (Gn 2:24, RSV). This verse describes marriage, a permanent union between one man and one woman. Permanence is indicated by the man "cleaving" to his wife (Hebrew *dabaq* [dah-BACK]), a word that means stuck or glued to something and not able to be removed (cf. 2 Samuel 23:10, RSV). That marriage is between one man and one woman (monogamy) is indicated by the man leaving "his father and mother" (not "fathers and mothers") in order to cleave to "his wife" (not "wives"), and that they become "one flesh" (not "several fleshes"). Indeed, we could translate this as "they become a single flesh," just one thing. This takes place in two ways. First, when they join together in the act of marriage, their bodies become a single unit designed to bring forth new life. Second, that new life itself comes equally from each of them—their bodies are literally joined together to make a single new body: a baby, a child. Surprisingly, by becoming *one*, they will become *many*. By joining as one flesh, they will be "fruitful and multiply, and fill the earth" as God commanded (Gn 1:28).

The story of the creation of man and woman (Gn 2:4–25) fits into the larger story of creation in seven days (Gn 1:1–2:3). All the events of Genesis 2 fit into the sixth and seventh day of Genesis 1. The creation of man and the animals (Gn 2:5–20) takes place on the sixth day. Adam falling into a deep sleep after a long day of naming animals (Gn 2:20) occurs on the night of the sixth day. When Adam awakes to behold Eve for the first time, that would be the morning of the seventh day. So the whole story of creation (Gn 1:1–2:25) climaxes with the revealing of the bride and Adam pronouncing the first-ever marriage vows (Gn 2:22–23). St. Thomas Aquinas points out that what is last in execution is first in intention.[1] In other words, the final step of a process is what you were hoping to achieve the whole time. For example, receiving your diploma on stage might be the last action of your high school career, but it was your goal from the beginning. So the marriage of Adam and Eve was the goal of all creation, even though it was the last action. And that marriage takes place on the seventh day, the Sabbath.

On the Sabbath day, God rested, and all creation rested with him. On the Sabbath day, everyone stops doing in order just to *be*. Specifically, to *be with* each other. God didn't create creatures for what they could do for him but to enjoy them and be with them, especially his highest creatures, human beings. We have a special term for *being with* another person: *communion*. God created humanity so that we could *commune* with him. So the Sabbath was the high point of the creation week, when God and humanity could commune with each other, enjoying each other's presence.

Many years ago, I was watching a TV comedy set in an American high school. A young man had a crush on a young woman, and every time she showed up, he engaged in silly antics to get her attention. Finally, she became annoyed and asked, "Why do you always act so crazy when I'm around?" He paused and dropped his guard, replying, "I just want to be with you." I was struck by that simple expression of communion—being with another person for their sake, to enjoy their presence, not for some other reason. At the heart of communion is love.

The Catholic faith teaches that God is a communion of three persons. The bond of love between the first two persons is so strong that it becomes the third person. Marriage is like that. The love of two persons becomes embodied in a third, the child. In this way, marriage becomes an image, an icon, of God. Love always wants to share itself. God creates other persons so that they can share his love and model his love. God created the world for loving communion, and the image of that communion is marriage. God created the world for marriage.

We can't go until we have drawn this stage of salvation history. Let's draw Mt. Eden first.

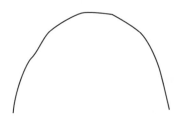

And add the River of Life.

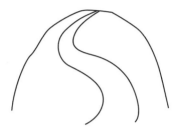

And the Tree of Life, with its four apples!

We know that the Tree of Life is a type of the Cross, and its fruit a type of the Eucharist. Likewise, the River of Life is a type of Baptism. We often talk about how these two life-giving sacraments were typified already in the garden, but we forget about a third life-giving sacrament that is also already there.

So let's begin to sketch in Adam. (You'll see why I'm waiting on his left arm in a minute.)

And now our lovely mother Eve! (Yes, I know she wasn't really wearing a dress, but just work with me here . . .)

And finally let's join their hands. This is the first marriage in history. We have the life-giving river, the life-giving tree, and the life-giving union of man and woman. The tree and river provided food and drink that could support eternal life. And the union of Adam and Eve produced persons in the image of the eternal God.

Let's make Adam and Eve smiling, as I'm sure they were very happy with each other and the garden before sin came in.

So here we have images of three life-giving sacraments. Sometimes we forget that marriage is meant to be life-giving, and we close it off to life. By doing so, we miss out on eternal joy that God intends for us.

There was no one else to serve as bridesmaids or groomsmen, so let's give them some angelic wedding attendants. Now our little picture is complete. This was how marriage should be: the happiness of communion, open to new life!

Two

Noah and His Wife

Sadly, Adam and Eve didn't stay in a state of happiness for long. God had placed Adam in the Garden of Eden to "work it and guard it" (Gn 2:15, my translation from Hebrew), but he didn't do a very good job of guarding, because at the beginning of Genesis 3, a snake has gotten into the garden and begins to confuse Eve. He persuades her to do the one thing God had forbidden: eating from the Tree of the Knowledge of Good and Evil. Then she shares the forbidden fruit with her husband (Gn 3:1–6).

This is the beginning of trouble, because it sows distrust in their covenant relationship with God. But the funny thing is, the covenant between God and *adam* is mysteriously connected to the marriage covenant between Adam and Eve. The two covenants resonate with each other, like two crystal glasses so similar that when you rub the rim of one, the other vibrates too. As a result, when Adam and Eve damage their covenant with God, they also damage their covenant with each other.

First, they realize they are naked (v. 7). To be naked is to be unprotected. Before, it didn't matter, as they had perfect trust in each other. But now, they are both cheaters who have broken trust with God, their loving Father. If they can break trust with him, they can break trust with each other. Now they don't feel safe in each other's presence. They make clothing of fig leaves to protect themselves from each other (v. 7).

God comes down to the garden to find the human couple and speak with them (v. 8). When what they've done comes to light, he declares the results of these actions for the serpent, the woman, and the man. One result is the disruption of the relationship of the man and woman. To the woman, God says, "Your desire shall be for your husband, and he shall rule over you" (v. 16). This is the beginning of the battle of the sexes. The woman will desire to control her husband, but she won't be successful. Before the first sin, there was no struggle for control because husband and wife were united in following the will of God. But now God's will has been set aside, and both want to impose their own will on the other.

Despite this sorrow, the story ends on a note of reconciliation. Adam gives his wife a new name, "Eve," the Hebrew word for "life," because she will be the mother of all the living (v. 20). He could have blamed her for their ill fortune and called her "bad luck" or "troublemaker," but instead, he gives her a beautiful and positive name, a celebration of the power of new life that she holds in her body. And God provides for the couple "garments of skins" to replace their ridiculous fig-leaf clothing (v. 21). Though they should have died upon eating the fruit (2:17), instead something else dies—an animal. God then uses the animal skins to give the man and woman clothing that is strong, durable, and comfortable. This establishes the pattern of sacrifice; animals will die in the place of man and woman, until a man comes who can die in the place of all mankind (see John 1:29).

Since they've broken faith with God, Adam and Eve cannot stay in the garden-temple of Eden. So they leave and begin their lives in a much less pleasant place (3:23–24). As they bear children, new problems arise. It is not long before we witness the first murder between brothers, when Cain murders Abel (Gn 4:8–16), but at least the divine model of marriage is honored for several generations. Then we come to Lamech, the sixth-generation descendant of Cain. Lamech was the first man to get a very bad idea: he took two wives (Gn 4:19). He was also a sociopath who bragged about his murders to his wives, and he boasted of being seven times worse than his ancestor Cain (vv. 23–24). The biblical narrator is trying to tell us something by letting us know bigamy was invented by such a wicked creep!

In the following generations, things go from bad to worse. In time, Lamech's bigamy blossoms into full-blown polygamy, as we read in Genesis 6:1–2: "When man began to multiply on the face of the land and daughters were born to them, the sons of God saw that the daughters of man were attractive. And they took as their wives any they chose" (ESV). "Any they chose" means "as many as they wanted." Catholic tradition understands the "sons of God" to be the covenant-keeping line of Seth, Adam and Eve's third son, since "son of God" is a term for one who keeps the covenant (cf. Ws 2:13–18). The "daughters of man" are the covenant-breaking line of Cain, who long ago turned from God. This polygamous intermarriage between covenant keepers and covenant breakers leads to a breakdown of human culture and the rise of violence. Things become so bad that it grieves God's heart; he created the world for loving communion, not for violence. So he sets in motion a great reboot, if you will, of human history. Choosing the most righteous man remaining, Noah, God commands Noah to build a ship (the ark) for himself, his family, and the animals, so that life will survive the great flood God will send.

Significantly, everyone that boards the ark is monogamous: Noah and his wife and Noah's three sons and their wives, eight people in all (Gn 7:13; see also 1 Peter 3:20). Even the animals are monogamous; each of them goes on the ark, as we all learned as children, "two by two." Notice the contrast shown here—outside the ark is polygamy and violence; inside the ark, there is monogamy and peace.

Polygamy does great damage to human society. It ruins the balance between man and wife that God intended. He made Eve to be *k'negdô*, "like and facing," paired and opposite. Spouses should see a reflection of themselves in their partner. But polygamous relationships *always* end up with multiple wives to one man, due to the nature of things. In such a situation, the husband can never fully return his wife's gaze of love because he is shared with other women. Moreover, fathers in polygamous relationships end up having too many children to teach, guide, and raise. Even if he tries, the man is stretched too thin, leaving kids with father absence. Added to that is the inevitable rivalry between wives and the psychological complex that kids get, knowing that their mother wasn't their father's "favorite." Every child has a right to be the product of true love, not just attraction. Every child deserves to be psychologically and spiritually secure, knowing his father and mother *did* and *do* love each other, and *only* each other, with a total, lifelong commitment. No favorites, no rivalries, no infidelities, no partial or temporary love—all those things hurt children as well as spouses. When fathers and mothers give themselves to each other completely and for life, the result is happy children and human flourishing.

Returning to the Flood story, we see that when Noah, his wife, and his sons and their wives come out of the ark, the world has been made new. Noah offers sacrifice, and God sends the rainbow as a sign of peace between himself and creation (Gn 8:20–9:17). In ancient times, warriors would hang their war bows over the hearth when a battle was over and they returned home. God hangs his "war bow" in the sky as a sign that the battle between earth and heaven is over (vv. 13, 16). He grants a new covenant to Noah and his family (vv. 9, 17). Noah and his wife are a new Adam and Eve, new parents of the human family. The proper covenant between God and humanity has been restored, and the proper covenant between man and woman has been restored, too. With this, we see once again how these two covenants are entwined with each other.

So we draw a new mountain, Ararat.

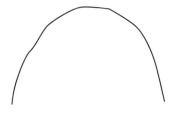

And here is the ark, a big, bargy boat.

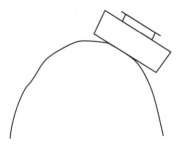

Let's let down the gangplank so some of these animals can get off.

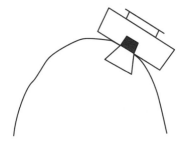

Here come the snakes, two by two.

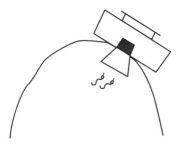

Now the giraffes, two by two.

And let's throw in some pairs of birds, for good measure.

And finally, the married couple, father and mother of a new humanity, Noah and his wife.

(We'll give Noah a captain's hat to tell him apart from Adam.)

On this whole scene, God sends his rainbow. They say that if you look down from the sky, rainbows are a perfect circle. Some call them "God's wedding ring." That seems very fitting, because the Flood is the triumph of monogamy.

Finally, we will make Mr. and Mrs. Noah smile, because this really is a happy scene: the restoration of balance and communion between God, humanity, and nature. What's not to like?

Three
Abraham and Sarah

You'd think after starting human history all over again with the most righteous man on earth that things would go well this time. But no! Only a few years after the Flood, Noah gets drunk on the wine of his own vineyard and passes out naked in his tent. His son Ham comes in and does something to shame him. Noah awakes from his drunkenness and puts a curse on some of Ham's descendants (Gn 9:20–27). So we have a case of the wrongful consumption of fruit leading to nakedness, shame, and a curse. It's the sin of the Garden of Eden all over again. Sin reenters the human family, and once more, things go from bad to worse. Finally, the whole human race joins together to defy God by building a great tower reaching up to the heavens. But God doesn't find it hard to put down this rebellion by his children. He merely confuses their languages, and the mob of rebels peacefully disperses over the face of the earth, as God had commanded them in the first place. But now we have the sorry situation that human beings are isolated from each other and separated from God. This defeats God's purpose in creating us—that humanity be one big happy family, the family of God.

So what can God do? He had sworn never again to send another flood. That option is off the table. God adopts a different strategy: he will work with one man and his family, and through them restore blessing to all of humanity. For this mission, he chooses a man named Abram. But Abram is a married man, and no less important for God's plan is Abram's wife, Sarai.

Abraham and Sarah

The Bible doesn't give us much background on Abram. He is already fairly old when God calls him and tells him: "Go from your country and your kindred and your father's house to the land that I will show you. And I will make of you a *great nation*, and I will bless you and make your *name great*, so that you will be a blessing. . . . and in you *all the families of the earth shall be blessed*" (Gn 12:1–3, ESV, emphasis added).

God makes Abram three major promises here: (1) that he would become a *great nation*, (2) that he would attain a *great name* (which means royalty), and (3) that through him would come a *great blessing* (blessing to all humanity). But the first promise—to become a great nation—was necessary for the rest to happen, and that was something Abram could not do by himself. His body did not have the power of life any more than Adam's did. Like Adam, Abram needed a life-giving "Eve," and that was his wife, Sarai.

But Abram doesn't seem to understand how important Sarai is to his future and God's promises. He passes her off as his sister, and she gets taken into the harem of a foreign king—not once but twice! (See Genesis 12:10–20 and 20:1–18.) God has to make direct intervention to protect

their marriage (Gn 12:17, 20:3). If he hadn't, those esca-
pades could have ended very badly for Abram and Sarai.
It's a sign of how important marriage is to God that when
Abram won't protect his marriage with Sarai, God steps
in to do it himself!
Yet God cannot save their marriage from self-inflicted
wounds. In Genesis 16, we find that many years have
elapsed since God promised to make Abram into a great
nation, and yet still Abram and Sarai have no children—
not a single one. Convinced that her childbearing years
are over, Sarai conceives a bad idea: she will give her lady's
maid, Hagar, to Abram as a second wife. By the laws of that
time, any children Hagar had would belong to Sarai. Sarai
is trying to force God's promises to come about through
some creative human effort. When Sarai shares her plan
with Abram, he "listened to the voice of Sar'ai" (Gn 16:2)—
the same phrase used when Adam followed Eve into sin
(Gn 3:17).

But do you remember the inventor of bigamy, Lamech?
Was he a good guy? Was it a good idea? No and no! And
bigamy certainly does not work out well for Abram,
Sarai, and Hagar. Instead, it brings grief to all three. As
expected, Hagar conceives and bears a son (Gn 16:4). Once
she becomes pregnant, Hagar gets proud and treats Sarai
with contempt (v. 4). Sarai retaliates by making Hagar's
life miserable (v. 6). This is what bigamy does—it destroys
the peace of the home. The situation becomes so intoler-
able that Hagar runs away, even though, in her pregnant
condition, there is really nowhere for her to go (v. 6). God
has to send an angel to reassure her that he will take care
of her and her child. With this reassurance, Hagar returns

home and puts up with the insufferable Sarai (vv. 7–14). In time, she bears the boy Ishmael (vv. 15–16).

But God is not pleased with Abram presiding over this train wreck. The plan of salvation has become completely derailed. God had promised to bless the fruit of the marriage of Abram and Sarai, not some third-party surrogate motherhood. If there is no intervention, the promises of the covenant will flow to Ishmael, the unintended son. Not that anything is wrong with Ishmael—God will bless him, too (Gn 17:20)—but the covenant was meant to pass to the son of Abram and Sarai.

God intervenes and appears once more to Abram, greeting him with a rebuke: "Walk before me, and be blameless" (Gn 17:1). This implies that Abram has not been blameless recently. Then God remakes the covenant between himself and Abram. When God first made the covenant with Abram in Genesis 15, Abram had to cut the flesh of animals (15:10). Now, however, God is going to have him cut his own flesh in the rite of circumcision. This ritual is a symbolic rebuke of Abram's powers of procreation, which he misused with Hagar. When he restates the terms of the covenant, God makes it crystal clear that the covenant promises will go to the son of Abram and Sarai (17:21).

Now, as I've said before, covenants form families. When you join a new family, you often get a new name. For example, we take a new name at Baptism and again at Confirmation. When God remakes his covenant with Abram in Genesis 17, both Abram and Sarai get new names. Sarai ("my princess") becomes Sarah ("princess"), and Abram ("exalted father") becomes Abraham ("father of a multitude"). Abraham's name seems ironic because he and Sarah still have no children together! The promise is wildly at odds with reality.

Nonetheless, God blesses Sarah in a special way: "She shall be a mother of nations; kings of peoples shall come from her" (Gn 17:16). When Abraham suggests God take it easy on himself and just bless Ishmael, God doubles down: "No, but Sarah your wife shall bear you a son, and you shall call his name Isaac. . . . I will establish my covenant with Isaac, whom Sarah shall bear to you at this season next year" (vv. 19, 21). It was always God's intention to bless their marriage with a child.

Within the year, God's promise comes to be. Abraham and Sarah become one flesh in the marital embrace, and then become one flesh in the body of a son, Isaac. For two old people to have a baby so late in life—to have to call an ob-gyn to the geriatrics ward!—is downright funny, so they name him Isaac (Hebrew, *yitzhāq* [hitz-HAHK]), meaning "laughter." It's God's big practical joke!

But Isaac's role in salvation history is no joke. He is the only son of Abraham and Sarah. The entire people of Israel, the Chosen People, will come from him. Isaac is the "only-begotten son" of Abraham and Sarah (Gn 22:2, 12, 16). Much like the "only-begotten Son" (Jn 3:16) who will come centuries later, Isaac as a young man will carry wood up a mountain and then lay himself on the wood to be sacrificed to God out of love for his father (Gn 22:1–14). This act will merit a blessing from God, such that God will solemnly swear to his father Abraham, "through your *seed* shall all the nations of the earth be blessed" (Gn 22:18, my translation, emphasis added). *Seed* (Hebrew *zera'* [zer-AH]) here means "descendant, son." Isaac is Abraham's first seed through whom blessing will come to the whole world.

Isaac and Rebekah

Well, with all that riding on Isaac's shoulders, it is critical that he marry a woman who suits him—who is capable of bearing with him the weight of the hopes of all humanity. That is why a long chapter of Genesis is devoted to the courtship of Rebekah (Gn 24). Abraham is concerned that Isaac find a wife who shares the same commitment to the same God that Abraham and his whole family worship. So Abraham commissions his steward, his most senior servant, to return to his homeland and choose a wife for Isaac from his relatives, who also worshipped the Lord (Gn 24:1–9). Abraham's servant sets off (v. 10), and on the way he strikes a deal with the Lord.

"Lord," the servant says, "I have to find a good wife for my master's son. You have to help me out, Lord. So this is what I'm going to do. When I come into town, I'm going to stop at the well for water. And when I ask a young woman for a drink, if she *volunteers* to water my camels, too, I'll know she's the one you want for Isaac!" (Gn 24:12–14, my paraphrase).

There's some common sense behind the servant's plan. Camels can drink up to thirty gallons at once, especially if they've been traveling for a while. The steward probably has at least half a dozen camels in his caravan. Any young woman who's going to *volunteer* to draw 180 gallons or more of water for a stranger's camels is not only kind and generous but also physically fit. Kind, generous, and strong—all good qualities for the future matriarch of Abraham's whole clan.

The steward rides into town, and the first woman he meets is Rebekah, a relative of Abraham and a beautiful, unmarried young woman. "Please give me a drink!" the steward says, and she responds, "Drink, my lord, and I will water your camels, too!" (Gn 24:17–19, my paraphrase). And she does. The steward heaps jewelry upon her and, after getting her family's blessing, takes her back to be the wife of Isaac (vv. 22–67). These two generous, self-giving people have a happy marriage. This episode, by the way, establishes "Give me a drink!" as a biblical pick-up line that we will encounter in romantic scenes later in the Bible as well.

Rebekah is vital to the history of salvation. The whole people of Israel come from her body. She also has the good sense to recognize that her younger son, Jacob (later called "Israel"), has the virtues to carry the covenant that her older son, Esau, does not. Esau (also called "Edom") is such a foolish lout that he sells his rights as firstborn to his younger brother in exchange for a bowl of soup, just because he's hungry and too lazy or impatient to make food for himself (see Genesis 25:29–34). Later in life, Isaac and Esau will attempt to ignore what Esau did, conspiring to give the firstborn blessing to Esau anyway, but thankfully, Rebekah intervenes to make sure Jacob's purchase of the firstborn rights is honored. She dresses him in Esau's clothes, puts hair skins on his arms, and sends him in to Isaac, who sees so poorly that he misidentifies Jacob as Esau by touch and smell. And so Isaac gives the covenant blessing to the one who had purchased it fairly from his foolish brother (Gn 27:1–40). Thus, because of Rebekah, the chosen people of God are the Israelites, not the Edomites. Through Isaac and Rebekah, the sacred author is showing us the importance of marriage, and the choice of one's spouse, for the future of God's people. The promises of the covenant include a "great nation," and that cannot come without many healthy descendants, and many healthy descendants can only come from healthy marriages.

Jacob and Rachel . . . and Leah

Of all the patriarchs, Isaac has the most peaceful life, because he only had one wife. Jacob, his heir, is not so lucky. As a young man, Jacob leaves home to return to Abraham's ancestral country, to seek a wife and life for himself. Coming to his mother Rebekah's hometown, he goes to the well and meets—you guessed it—a beautiful, unmarried young woman, Rachel (Gn 29:1–14). He falls in love at first sight. With no money to his name, he promises to work for Rachel's father, Laban (Rebekah's brother), for seven years to earn the money for her bride price. (Young men paid a girl's father a large sum of money for the privilege of her hand in marriage back in those days. It was an excellent practice that I, as the father of three daughters, heartily approve!) But the years fly by because of Jacob's love, and at last the two can get married (vv. 15–20).

But then Laban does something wicked that makes three basically good and decent young people miserable for the rest of their lives. He takes his unmarried, less-pretty older daughter, Leah, and slips her into the bridal chamber on Jacob's wedding night. In the morning, Jacob wakes up and gets a good look at his wife and it's Leah! As we can well imagine, he exchanges some choice words with Laban, but what's done is done. Jacob cannot unmarry Leah. He can and does marry Rachel, however, a week later, and now he has two sisters as wives—a situation so bad that Moses will later make it illegal (Lv 18:18).

Laban is the rascal in this whole affair. Jacob did not want more than one wife. He only wanted Rachel. Neither did Rachel or Leah want to be part of a polygamous marriage. They were all pawns in Laban's plan to foist both of his daughters on his nephew. It's a recipe for great unhappiness. Leah knows she is unloved, but God blesses her with children (Gn 29:30–34). Rachel has Jacob's love but no children (30:1). Leah envies Rachel's love, and Rachel envies Leah's fertility. They fight over their husband and begin a "baby war," taking a page from Sarah's playbook and pressing their lady's maids, Bilhah and Zilpah, into action as surrogate mothers (30:3–24). In a certain way, all these shenanigans do *something* good—Jacob ends up with twelve sons! But they are from four different mothers, and most of the sons feel keenly the fact that their father did not really love their mother. This creates rivalry between the sons of different mothers, and most of the hatred ends up focused on Joseph, the oldest son of Rachel, the only wife Jacob ever loved or wanted to marry.

We all know the story of Joseph. His brothers hate him so much they first try to kill him; then they decide to sell him as a slave (Gn 37:1–28). But Joseph, surprisingly, turns out to be a young man of great faith and integrity. His virtues and his prophetic gifts enable him to rise from Egyptian slavery to the position of royal steward in the house of Pharaoh (Gn 39–41). But when famine drives his brothers to Egypt to buy grain, Joseph can't resist getting some revenge (Gn 42–44). He plays with his brothers and, while not doing them any real harm, makes their lives miserable until finally Judah—the very brother that sold him into slavery—steps forward and offers his own life in exchange for the life of Benjamin, Joseph's younger and only full brother (44:18–34). That act of selflessness breaks through the bitterness, envy, and resentment that has estranged the brothers and opens the path to reconciliation (Gn 45). So the book of Genesis ends well, with the brothers overcoming their resentments and all moving their families down to Egypt, where they will live as one big happy family—at least for a while (Gn 46–50).

But notice what the sacred author has shown us along the way: God's creation culminated in marriage. Marriage is the only way God's intentions for humanity can be fulfilled. God's plan for marriage before the Fall was one man and one woman together for life. Bigamy was the evil invention of that psychopath Lamech. Polygamy is so bad it led to the Flood. Everyone saved in the ark—both man and animal—was monogamous. When the patriarchs strayed outside of monogamy, bad things happened. No patriarch ever wanted polygamy—it was pushed on them by others (their wives or Laban). The rivalry among sons set up by polygamy almost ruined the family of Jacob. Only Judah's selflessness toward his brother from a different mother (Benjamin) saved the family.

When people ask, "Why does the Bible approve of polygamy? Didn't the patriarchs have more than one wife?" they're responding to a very simplistic reading. Folks don't read slowly and carefully enough to pick up the message that God is trying to send us. The message is: stick with one spouse! That leads to happiness.

Now it's time to sketch a stick-figure icon that can capture some of the main ideas about the marriages of the patriarchs and matriarchs. Obviously, we can't sketch them all. So I will focus on Isaac and Rebekah. They are the central pair of the three sets of patriarchs and matriarchs. They also lived out matrimony the best of all of them.

We start with a well.

This is where Isaac and Rebekah met. Well, sort of. Isaac courted Rebekah by proxy, which seems kind of strange now. But it worked.

Next we sketch in Isaac.

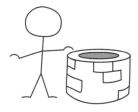

Yes, I know he is handsome, but we are not focusing on looks at the moment. We have more serious things to consider, like the nature of self-sacrifice. So under Isaac's right hand we are going to draw a ram. This is the ram that took Isaac's place on the altar at the top of Mt. Moriah. This reminds us of the *aqedah*, the binding of Isaac on the altar when he willingly offered himself as a sacrifice to God. This is the closest experience to the Cross that we encounter in the Old Testament. The ram is a reminder of Isaac's willingness to give himself completely.

This is what made Isaac and Rebekah such a good couple. They were both generous, willing to give themselves to the full.

Let's start sketching in Rebekah.

Then we will add the symbol of Rebekah's self-giving: her water jar.

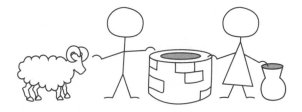

We better add a rope so she can lift it up from the well.

It was her water jar that won Rebekah her role as bride of Isaac, princess of the tribe, and grand-matriarch of Israel. Rebekah was a generous soul who would give of herself even when it hurt.

Both Isaac and Rebekah remind us of Jesus. Isaac carried the wood of his sacrifice on his back up a mountainside. On the top, he was laid on the wood to be sacrificed to God out of love for his father, as Jesus would do on Calvary. Rebekah was willing to produce probably 180 gallons of water by her own strength simply because she saw that a stranger was in need and thirsty. Likewise, when Jesus was a guest at a wedding at Cana, he produced 180 gallons of fine wine to satisfy the thirst of all the strangers at the party with him. Jesus would end his life by asking for a drink (Jn 19:28), trying to see if there was anyone who would be a "Rebekah" for him. But none stepped up. All he got was a damp sponge of vinegar.

Isaac and Rebekah understood what St. John Paul II called "The Law of the Gift."[2] It is in giving ourselves completely, St. John Paul II taught, that we discover ourselves and grow in love. And when we find another person that practices that same self-giving love, it can be a beautiful thing. Marriage calls for a total self-gift of each spouse to the other. When both live that out well, it leads to a lot of

happiness because—whether they know it or not—both
spouses are being like Jesus.

Four

God and Israel at Sinai

When we start the book of Exodus, we get some good news. After all the struggles with infertility that the grandfathers and grandmothers of Israel had (Gn 11:30, 25:21, 29:31), finally the descendants of Abraham have been "fruitful" and "multiplied" and "filled" the land (Ex 1:7). God's command and blessing to Adam and Eve in Genesis 1:28 has been fulfilled by the people of Israel.

God had promised Abraham that he would become a "great nation" (Gn 12:2). His descendants have now become numerous enough to be a nation, but there are two other things they need: laws and land. To meet those needs, God sends them a deliverer, Moses.

It seems like God's original plan to deliver Israel was for Moses to be adopted into Pharaoh's household. Then, in time, he would rise to power and have his people freed legally and peacefully. We could call this God's Plan A.

If Moses had kept his head down and bided his time, Plan A would have worked. As it was, he lost his temper, killed an Egyptian officer, and botched the disposal of the body (Ex 2:11–15). He was outed as an Israelite sympathizer, and he had to flee from Pharaoh's court to the far side of

the eastern desert, to a country of sheepherders known
as Midian. There he sat down by a well and—you guessed
it—met his future wife, Zipporah, who went on to bear
him two sons (vv. 15–22).

You might think the marriage theme in the Bible would
continue with Moses, since he meets his wife so much
like Isaac and Jacob did. But actually, the Bible spends
very little time on Moses's marriage. Instead, the marriage
theme pivots in Exodus, and the bride and groom become
the people and God, for the first time in the Bible.

As we all know—since we've all watched Cecil B.
DeMille's *Ten Commandments* with Charlton Heston or
DreamWorks's *Prince of Egypt*—Moses leads the people of
Israel out of Egypt and through the Red Sea to Mt. Sinai,
where God meets with the people and shows his presence
in the form of a great storm over the mountain. Events
then unfold like a marriage ceremony. Moses plays the role
of the clergyman or justice of the peace who officiates at
the marriage. He receives from God the Ten Commandments (Ex 20) and some other basic laws (Ex 21–23) that
are terms of the covenant, the solemn family relationship
between God and Israel. These laws can also be compared
to a marriage contract.

Moses reads all the laws to Israel, so that the people
know what their rights and responsibilities are as "spouse"
of God. The people respond with a solemn vow: "All the
words which the LORD has spoken we will do" (Ex 24:3).
Then, Moses completes the "betrothal" of God to Israel.
He takes the blood of sacrificed animals and sprinkles
half on God's altar and half on the people. That the people
and God each receive half the blood indicates they are
entering equally into this marriage-like covenant. The

blood has two meanings. One is kinship: God and Israel are now family; they share one blood. The other meaning is a curse. The sprinkled blood means, "May my blood be shed if I don't keep the commitment I am making in this ceremony."[3]

After a wedding, there's usually a reception with a big meal, and at Sinai we see that, too. When the solemn vows and ceremony are over, seventy leaders of the people climb Mt. Sinai with Moses and share a meal with the Lord. The Bible says, "They beheld God, and ate and drank" (Ex 24:11). Later Jewish tradition understood this to mean that they looked at God, and in this way they ate and drank. In other words, the vision of God was their food and drink. It was a foretaste of heaven, when we will all see God face-to-face. The Church calls that "the beatific vision."

Israel was now "married" to God by this covenant ceremony that Moses had celebrated for them. In ancient times, after a betrothal ceremony, the bridegroom often went to prepare a place for himself and his new bride to live, and then returned to take her to live with him. In Exodus, we see something like this. After the "betrothal" of God with Israel at Sinai, Moses goes back up the mountain to receive instructions for the tabernacle, the portable sanctuary where God will live with his bridal people.

The honeymoon, however, doesn't last very long. After forty days, the people of Israel get impatient waiting for Moses to come down the mountain, and they completely give up on their new relationship with God. They go to Moses's brother, Aaron, and say, "Up, make us gods, who shall go before us; as for this Moses . . . we do not know what has become of him" (Ex 32:1). Aaron makes them a golden idol of a calf, perhaps an image of the bull god

Apis, whom they would have worshipped in Egypt. The people hailed it as a god and offered sacrifices to it. Then they "sat down to eat and drink, and rose up to play" (32:6). The word "play" here is a polite way of saying they began to do in public things that should only be done by spouses in private. We see here the same biblical pattern we have talked about before: when people break covenant with God, they usually break the covenant of marriage, too. The sin with the calf involved both spiritual adultery with a false god and physical adultery among the people.

When the people of Israel made the covenant with the Lord, they received the sprinkled blood, which meant, "May my blood be shed if I do not keep my commitments." With their latest actions, they had called down a curse of death on themselves. And it was up to God to enforce the curse they had sworn. So on the mountain, while Moses and God are conversing, God suddenly says to Moses, "Let me alone, that my wrath may burn hot against them" (Ex 32:10). But Moses intercedes for the people, and in response to his prayers, God grants them forgiveness. Moses goes down to the camp, punishes those who were leading this riotous party, and regains control of the people. He pleads with God once more, and God renews the covenant with Israel—but not without some additional laws designed to make sure something like the calf rebellion did not happen again.

Moses proceeds to build the tabernacle according to all the instructions that God had given him while he was on the mountain. At the end of the book of Exodus, the tabernacle is completed, and the presence of God comes down and fills the whole tabernacle with glory. So Exodus ends on a beautiful note: despite the people's unfaithfulness,

God the bridegroom comes down to live with Israel his bride in their common home, the tabernacle.

We should say something about the laws of marriage that Moses established for the people of Israel. Most of these are designed to protect the union of bodies that is at the heart of marriage. God designed that sacred union to symbolize the total and permanent commitment of spouses to each other. Because of this, sexual union should never take place when that total and permanent commitment isn't there—for example, between people not married to each other (Ex 20:14), people not married at all (Ex 22:16–17), or people who can't and shouldn't marry each other for some reason (Lv 18, 20). Late in his life, after struggling unsuccessfully for forty years to make the Israelites follow God's law, Moses lowered these standards. In the book of Deuteronomy, recorded at the end of Moses's life, he gave the Israelites laws that quietly allowed for polygamy (Dt 21:15–16) and divorce (Dt 24:1–4). Jesus later explains that Moses did this because of Israel's "hardness of heart" (Mt 19:7–9).

The Israelites had trouble keeping their covenant commitments. They broke their covenant with the Lord not only in the golden calf incident (Ex 32) but ten more times while wandering in the wilderness for forty years. Likewise, they couldn't keep their covenant commitments to their wives. So Moses, worn out after decades of struggle, reluctantly gave up and allowed marriages to be broken even though, as Jesus points out, this was not God's original plan (Mt 19:8). Yet even at the end of Moses's life, in Deuteronomy, he was still giving laws that pointed to the goodness and joy that God intended for marriage. For example, Moses commanded that a newlywed man could not be drafted into the army or given any other business, so that he could be free at home for one year to bring joy to his wife (Dt 24:5, NABRE). Later rabbis would understand from this that one of the sacred duties of a husband was to make his wife happy. That was God's original intention—that marriage would bring love and joy to spouses.

God is the perfect spouse, and he intended love and joy for his bride, Israel. Even God's laws were not given to Israel to burden or restrict her but that "you may live, and that it may go well with you, and that you may live long in the land which you shall possess" (Dt 5:33). So let's begin to sketch in the "marriage" of God and Israel at Sinai.

We can start by drawing Sinai.

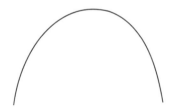

That was easy. The rest will be harder, though.

How do we represent the celebration of a nuptial covenant between the unseen creator God and the entire nation of Israel? I'm going to do my best. Don't be too judgmental!

I'm going to start by placing Moses on Mt. Sinai.

Moses plays a special part in this marriage covenant. His role is to arrange the marriage and accept the vows between the parties, like the minister in most modern weddings. Ministers usually carry a Bible or book of prayers, so we will put the Ten Commandments in Moses's hands—the closest thing to a Bible available in his day.

Now, we sketch the groom. This groom is divine and cannot be portrayed in any earthly form. We will represent him as he appeared at Sinai, showing his glory through a great storm at the top of the mountain.

Now, the bride. The bride here is the entire people of Israel, who formed a large crowd at the foot of the mountain. Drawing a crowd at first seems daunting but actually is not so bad.

We can get away with three Israelites, because everyone knows that three's a crowd.

But it's not quite good enough, because we need to mark the people of Israel as the bride, so let's give the Israelites veils and bouquets.

And there you have it: the nuptial covenant being formed
between God and his people at Sinai, with Moses serving
as minister.

God's faithfulness to this covenant for the rest of history will serve as the model for all human marriages.

Five

Boaz and Ruth

Moses, of course, never did succeed in getting the people to the Promised Land. That was left to his successor, Joshua. The story of Israel's conquest and settlement of their land is told in the book that bears Joshua's name. After Joshua's death, however, Israel plunged into a dark time where moral and social chaos was normal, and the people were often at the mercy of their enemies. Periodically, God would send them a savior figure, a "judge," who would lead them to victory over their enemies and establish a temporary peace. So we call this the era of the judges, narrated in the book of the same name.

The theme of the book of Judges is stated clearly twice: "In those days there was no king in Israel; every man did what was right in his own eyes" (Jgs 17:6, 21:25). This means there was no central authority, so everyone did what they felt like. The result was chaos. A lot of people were hurt, particularly women. One of the victims of this chaotic period was respect for women and marriage. In fact, the book of Judges ends with a shocking story depicting this loss of respect. The story starts with one woman being raped and killed by a mob and ends with hundreds of young women being kidnapped and forced to marry (Jgs 19–21).

Why are such stories in the Bible? For one, the Bible is a realistic book, and awful things such as these did happen and continue to happen in the world. And also, the point is that we *should* be shocked by a story like this. It illustrates what can happen in a country (or a church) when there is no clear moral authority and everyone does what they want.

However, there were some bright spots in this time of darkness. One of them was the little town of Bethlehem, the town where two great kings would be born: David and, much later, Jesus. Even in the time of the judges, Bethlehem was a place where people loved God, followed his laws, and practiced respect for women and marriage. We see that in one of the shortest and most beautiful books of the Bible, Ruth.

The book of Ruth begins with a crisis. There is a famine in Israel. It is so bad that a certain man from Bethlehem named Elimelech has to move to the land of Moab to find food for his wife and two sons (Ru 1:1–2). This is ironic, because "Bethlehem" means "house [*beth*] of bread [*lehem*]." Things were so bad there was no bread in the House of Bread! Not only that, but Moab was a long-standing enemy of the people of Israel. An Israelite from Bethlehem moving to Moab for food would be like a corn farmer from Nebraska having to move to Russia to feed his family during the height of the Cold War.

Things don't work out too well in Moab. Elimelech's family lives there for a decade, but in that time Elimelech dies, followed by his two sons, leaving his wife and two daughters-in-law as widows (vv. 3–5). Elimelech's widow,

Naomi, hears that the famine is over in Bethlehem and decides to return to her hometown. Her daughters-in-law want to go with her, but she urges them not to; they are from Moab, and there's no future for them in Bethlehem (vv. 6–15). But her daughter-in-law Ruth refuses to leave Naomi. She says: "Entreat me not to leave you or to return from following you; for where you go I will go, and where you lodge I will lodge; your people shall be my people, and your God my God; where you die I will die, and there will I be buried. May the LORD do so to me and more also if even death parts me from you" (Ru 1:16–17, RSV).

This is strong language. It is actually a covenant-making oath. You may remember that we said a covenant is the extension of kinship by oath. Ruth is swearing to be Naomi's daughter no matter what happens, on pain of death. And by becoming Naomi's daughter, she is also accepting Naomi's people and her God. It's quite dramatic. Ruth is going all in as an Israelite daughter to Naomi. In a special way, Ruth has thrown herself into the care of the God of Israel, which sets up the tension of the story: Is the God of Israel going to come through for her?

The two women arrive in Bethlehem and set up a house for themselves (1:19–22). Naomi is too old to work, so Ruth knows it will be up to her to provide for the two of them. There were not many ways for women to support themselves in those days, but she could *glean*—that is, follow harvesters in the field and collect any dropped or leftover grain. As fate would have it, she ends up gleaning in the field of Boaz, a wealthy relative of Naomi's (2:1–3).

And soon our hero, Boaz, shows up in person (2:4). The name "Boaz" means "in him is strength." Great name for a guy. He's also wealthy and a relative of Ruth's deceased husband and father-in-law. In ancient Israel, if a woman's husband died, it was law that her husband's nearest brother or kinsman marry her, so she could have a home and children of her own (Dt 25:5–10). The nearest kinsman had the right and obligation to marry the widow. He was called a "redeemer"—in Hebrew, a *gō'ēl* [go-ALE]. Boaz was a redeemer. So all of this is great. As soon as Boaz shows up, we know he is "the goods."

The first thing out of Boaz's mouth is the name of God: "The LORD be with you!" he calls to his workers (2:4). They respond: "The LORD bless you" (2:5). It sounds like Mass! Boaz and his workers take God seriously and are committed to their faith.

Boaz cannot help noticing the new young woman gleaning in the field—after all, Bethlehem was a small town where everyone knew each other. When he finds out how she gave up her former life to care for her mother-in-law, he is truly impressed. He goes over to her and welcomes her to his field, inviting her to stay on his property, where he will make sure she is safe and the young men don't tease or flirt with her (2:5–11). In fact, he even calls down a blessing on her: "A full reward be given you by the LORD, the God of Israel, under whose wings you have come to take refuge!" (Ru 2:12, RSV).

Ruth is very appreciative. At lunchtime, Boaz invites her to eat with him and the workers. Afterwards, he tells his men to throw extra grain on the ground for her to pick up. He is really watching out for her (2:14–16). It doesn't take long for Naomi, the clever mother-in-law, to realize that Boaz likes Ruth and that Ruth doesn't mind his attentions, either. Naomi is not one to leave things to chance, so she comes up with a plan to get the two of them together—and alone. "Isn't Boaz having a harvest party at the town threshing floor tonight?" Naomi asks Ruth (3:2, my paraphrase). Then she instructs her daughter-in-law: "Wash therefore and anoint yourself, and put on your best clothes and go down to the threshing floor; but do not make yourself known to the man until he has finished eating and drinking. But when he lies down, observe the place where he lies; then, go and uncover his feet and lie down; and he will tell you what to do" (Ru 3:3–4, RSV). This is a bit forward, to say the least! It's like telling Ruth: "Put on your little black dress, heels, and best perfume. Hang out at the party until he lies down on the couch, then snuggle up to him and see what happens!"

The sacred author tells the story of what happens next so well that there's no way to improve on his words: "She went down to the threshing floor and did just as her mother-in-law had instructed her. Boaz ate and drank to his heart's content, and went to lie down at the edge of the pile of grain. She crept up, uncovered a place at his feet, and lay down. Midway through the night, the man gave a start and groped about, only to find a woman lying at his feet. 'Who are you?' he asked. She replied, 'I am your servant Ruth. Spread the wing of your cloak over your servant, for you are a redeemer'" (Ru 3:6–9, NABRE).

Oh, my goodness, this is really intense! This is the point of the movie where you reach over to cover your kids' eyes and say to yourself, "I thought this was rated PG!" Ruth is making a big-time play for Boaz in the middle of the night, after he's had a good bit to drink at a party. What's going to happen?

Let's especially notice that she asks him to throw the "wing" (that is, the flap) of his cloak over her. That was

a very important gesture in ancient Israel. A man typi-
cally would only throw his cloak over a woman in a public
betrothal ceremony (see Ezekiel 16:8). It meant he was
taking her as his wife and pledging to clothe, feed, care
for, and protect her and her children for life. Ruth is asking
Boaz to marry her, and she has made herself as tempting
to him as possible. Boaz is in line to marry her according
to Israel's law, anyway: "You are [my] redeemer" (Ru 3:9,
NABRE). But let's note that the word "wing" only shows
up twice in this book. In chapter 2, Boaz blessed Ruth by
the Lord, under whose "wings" she had taken refuge (2:12).
Now, Ruth is asking Boaz to be the "wing" of the Lord to
care for her and protect her.

It's true there was a moral and legal reason for Boaz
to marry Ruth, but in the middle of the night on a public
threshing floor was not the proper place to celebrate a
wedding! Things could have really spun out of control if
Boaz hadn't been such a good guy. But even in the dark of
night, after having had a fair amount to drink, and with
a very attractive and inviting young woman lying beside
him, Boaz still thinks clearly and does the right thing:
"May you be blessed by the LORD, my daughter; you have
made this last kindness greater than the first, in that you
have not gone after young men, whether poor or rich" (Ru
3:10, RSV). From this we learn that Boaz is touched that
she would offer herself to him. He must have liked her but
figured she wouldn't have him because he wasn't a young
man anymore. But look at how, even in this compromising
situation, the first words out of his mouth are a blessing
from the Lord! I love Boaz; he's such a great guy.

The story wraps up quickly and sweetly. Boaz agrees to
marry Ruth, provided the legal details work out (3:10–13).

He loads Ruth up with grain to bring home to Naomi and sends her away before dawn so that her reputation won't be tarnished. He didn't want her to be known as the kind of girl who would sneak down to the threshing floor to crash a guys' party (vv. 14–18). The following morning, there's one snag he has to tend to: technically, there is another relative in the family who has first claim on Ruth and her deceased husband's property. Boaz finds the man and confronts him with the situation at the city gate (4:1–4). Thankfully, this man is already married and not interested in complicating his life (vv. 5–6). The path is now clear for Boaz to marry Ruth, and he wastes no time. They are soon married and have a little boy together, Obed (4:7–13). Naomi is overjoyed and becomes his nurse. In time, Obed becomes the father of Jesse, and Jesse, the father of David (vv. 13–22). So Ruth the Moabitess becomes the great-grandmother of the king of Israel and ancestress of Jesus, King of the World.

The book of Ruth conveys two important messages. One message is that God provides hope in hard times. Even in all the chaos of the time of the judges, there were still some places like Bethlehem where people loved the Lord and followed his laws, including special rules to take care of the poor and vulnerable, such as widows and orphans. Also, by trusting in the Lord and following his law, Ruth and Boaz were drawn to each other, found happiness, and started a family. Their marriage and family provided an answer for the terrible times they were living through, because their great-grandson would be the one to finally put an end to the chaos and make Israel into a great kingdom.

We are also living in a very difficult time, when marriage is disappearing, family life is falling apart, and loneliness is rising—even in the Church. But God can still work through humble people who love him, love each other, and follow God's plan for marriage. The future lies with God-fearing couples like Boaz and Ruth.

A second message is that when we are faithful to God and his laws, God will lead us to our true vocation. Boaz and Ruth had a vocation to marriage—specifically, to be married to each other. But they would never have found each other if they hadn't first been faithful to the Lord, the God of Israel. If Ruth hadn't sworn an oath to be faithful to Naomi, her people, and her God, she would have gone back to Moab the way her sister-in-law, Orpah, did. There would have been no marriage to Boaz, no David, no book of Ruth, etc. Likewise, if Boaz hadn't followed the laws of God, which commanded special care and compassion for widows and migrants (Dt 24:19–22), he wouldn't have ended up with Ruth. By following God, they were led to each other. That is an excellent way to find a spouse.

The church fathers saw Boaz as a *type* (that is, an image or foreshadowing) of Christ, one "in whom is strength," who provides his bride with the "finest of the wheat" (Ps 81:16), the Eucharist. And Ruth is a type of the Church, who puts her faith in God and so finds a loving bridegroom who provides her with spiritual food and fruitfulness. Finally, Boaz and Ruth's great-grandson David would be another important type of Jesus, bridegroom of the Church.

So let's sketch out our icon of Boaz and Ruth. (This should be a little easier than God and Israel at Sinai!)

First, let's sketch in Ruth.

Let's give her a sheaf of wheat, so we can tell her from the other great women of salvation history.

Next, let's draw in her husband, Boaz.

His hand is outstretched, ready to hold a flail.

Flails were two heavy sticks bound with a leather strap, used to thresh grain. They symbolized the ability to provide food for others. Boaz is the great "breadwinner" of the book of Ruth. Interestingly, flails were also associated with royalty, because a good king made sure there was plenty of food for his people. This reminds us that Boaz is the father of kings. Speaking of fatherhood, let's get little Obed into this picture:

After all, Ruth and Boaz's marriage wasn't just about themselves; like marriage in general, its goal was to raise a family.

Obed in turn would father Jesse, who would father David, the founder of the royal dynasty. Even though it's a little early, we will put a small crown on Obed to stand for the dynasty that comes from his line.

In this image we see many types. The grain is a type of the Eucharist. Just as Boaz uses the wood of his flail to produce grain to feed and nourish Ruth, so Christ will use the wood of the Cross to provide his body as our true "grain" to satisfy the Church. Boaz also makes Ruth fruitful herself, able to bear a child, as Jesus makes us able to bear the fruit of good works and souls won for him. This image reminds us of the close tie between the sacraments of Matrimony and Eucharist, as both involve the gift and union of bodies, which brings forth new life.

Six

Solomon and His Bride

The Song of Songs

The children of Boaz and Ruth continued to live in Bethlehem and love the Lord as their parents did. Their grandson Jesse became a prosperous farmer, and it was his eighth and youngest son that the prophet Samuel chose to be king over all Israel. When Samuel came to the house of Jesse and anointed the young David with oil, "the Spirit of the LORD rushed upon David from that day forward" (1 Sm 16:13, ESV). David is the only person in the Old Testament who had the continuous presence of the Holy Spirit.

Of course, when David was anointed king by Samuel, Israel already had a king: the troubled Saul, who had started out so well but then wandered from the Lord. David bided his time, putting up with Saul's abuse until the collapse of his reign. Then all the people of Israel came to realize that David was their best choice for king. The Bible describes it this way: "Then all the tribes of Israel came to David at Hebron, and said, 'Behold, *we are your bone and flesh.*' . . . So all the elders of Israel came to the king at Hebron; and King David made a *covenant* with them at Hebron before the LORD, and they anointed David king over Israel" (2 Sm 5:1–3, RSV, emphasis added).

The declaration, "We are your bone and flesh," is covenant-making language, calling to mind the marriage covenant between Adam and Eve (Gn 2:23). Significantly, the tribes of Israel do *not* say to David, "You are *our* bone and flesh," claiming David as their own, as Adam claimed Eve. That is the role of the bridegroom. Instead, they adopt the role of the bride: "We are *your* bone and flesh." In other words, "Take us, we belong to you!" similar to Ruth's proposal to Boaz (see Ruth 3:9). David agrees and makes a covenant with the people. This was not a literal marriage, of course, but it was like a marriage, in which the king was husband to the people. The king was supposed to protect, provide, care for, and love the people. And the people were to love and follow the king in return.

The marriage-like relationship between a king and his people shows up elsewhere in the Bible. For example, much later in David's career, his son Absalom overthrows him. Absalom makes himself king in Jerusalem, but David flees to the east with his loyal soldiers. The royal counselor Ahithophel gives Absalom some advice: "Let me choose twelve thousand men, and I will set out and pursue David tonight. . . . I will strike down the king only, and I will bring all the people back to you *as a bride comes home to her husband*" (2 Sm 17:1–3, emphasis added). Here again we see that the king was a husband to the people as bride.

This romantic relationship between king and people does not reach its height under David but under David's son and heir, Solomon. Solomon is the great romantic hero of the Old Testament, because he is the subject of the

Bible's great love poem, the Song of Solomon, also known as the Song of Songs.

The Song of Songs has got to be the most unusual book in the entire Old Testament. It's in a class by itself; nothing else is like it. People react to it strongly and in different ways—some find it offensive, others find it comical, and many saints found it to be the most profound and mystical of all the Old Testament works. How can one book provoke such different reactions? What is the Song of Songs?

The Song of Songs is a collection of love poems focusing on Solomon and his bride, arranged with a loose plot. Most of the poems are surreal fantasy. They don't describe real events but dreams or daydreams of Solomon's bride as her wedding day approaches. The poems are written as dialogues, with speaking parts for the bride, the groom, and a chorus composed of the bride's girlfriends, called "the daughters of Jerusalem." In fact, the whole Song of Songs can be performed as a musical or a light opera, with a man, a woman, and a choir singing the different parts.

The Song opens with a *colloquy*, part of a play or musical where many people speak together (Sg 1:1–2:7). We are introduced to the bride, the groom, and the chorus. The bride announces that she is being brought into the king's chambers, together with her girlfriends (bridesmaids)—in other words, a royal wedding is about to take place (Sg 1:1–4). Then the bride and groom trade compliments with each other, pretending to be a shepherd and shepherdess, probably flirtatious role-playing (1:5–2:5). From time to time, the chorus of girlfriends chimes in as the young couple profess their love for each other (1:4, 11). Finally, the scene concludes with the bride saying:

> O that his left hand were under my head,
>   and that his right hand embraced me!
> I adjure you, O daughters of Jerusalem,
>   by the gazelles or the hinds of the field,
> that you stir not up nor awaken love until it [literally,
>   "she"] please. (Sg 2:6–7, RSV, note added)

Surprise! We thought the bridegroom was right there with her. So why does she wish he was there embracing her? The clue is in the next sentence, which has a double meaning. It can be translated as above, or this way: "I adjure you . . . that you stir not up nor awaken the Loved One until she please" (Sg 2:6–7). That's because the same Hebrew word ('*ahabah* [AH-hah-VAH]) can mean either "love" or else "loved one," "beloved," or "my love" (as in 7:6). So she's really saying two things: don't arouse the passions of love before their time, and also, don't *wake me up* until I want to, until it's time for the wedding. The bride is the loved one, as the bridegroom calls her in Song 7:6. For much of the Song she is sleeping and dreaming—sometimes daydreaming—about her upcoming wedding and honeymoon.

After this opening colloquy (Song 1:1–2:7), we have a kind of daydream in which the groom bounds down from the hills to come outside the bride's garden and invite her to run off to the hills with him to enjoy the birds and flowers of the springtime (2:8–17). Then we have an actual dream sequence, in which the bride is in her bed at night and dreams of going out into the city to find her beloved (3:1–5). When she finds him, she embraces him and brings him back home. The dream ends with the bride repeating her command not to wake up the loved one until she please.

At the center of the Song of Songs is a grand vision of Solomon and his bride being carried into Jerusalem in the royal palanquin or litter, a kind of luxurious mobile bedchamber carried on poles by royal bodyguards (Sg 3:6–5:1). First, we see the royal litter carrying Solomon up from the eastern wilderness into the royal city Jerusalem (3:6–11). Then, we enter the litter and hear the intimate conversation between Solomon and his bride. He flatters her and describes all her beauty, from head to toe, in flowery poetry (Sg 4:1–15). She responds by inviting him to come and embrace her (4:16). He approaches her (5:1a), and the curtain drops to give the newlyweds privacy, as the chorus of bridesmaids chants well wishes over the young couple (5:1b).

What follows is another dream sequence (5:2–6:10) with the same basic plot as the earlier one (3:1–5) but told in much greater detail. The bride is in her bed, dreaming. In her dream, her beloved is knocking on her chamber, but when she opens the door, he has gone. She runs out into the city by night to look for him, but she cannot find him. She runs into her girlfriends. They offer to help look, and she provides a detailed description of her beloved (5:10–16). This description gets the girlfriends interested! They start to search, but the search is quickly over (6:1). The bride finds her beloved, and they exchange romantic compliments and sweet nothings as the chorus chimes in (6:2–9).

Abruptly, the bride is awake, and we find her walking to the orchard, where she suddenly has a vivid daydream (6:11–12). In her fantasy, her royal boyfriend rides up in his chariot and takes her on board (v. 12). As they ride off together, he heaps her with compliments, describing her beautiful features from her toes to the top of her head (7:1–9). She invites him to take her out into the countryside where they can enjoy each other's company alone among the quiet vineyards (7:10–13). The daydream ends with the familiar formula:

> O that his left hand were under my head,
>> and that his right hand embraced me!
> I adjure you, O daughters of Jerusalem,
>> that you stir not up nor awaken the Loved One
>>> until she please. (8:3–4, RSV; last line, alternate translation)

This lets us know that this, too, was but a dream.

The Song ends with a final colloquy in which everyone wakes up and speaks (8:5–14). The bride offers some reflections on the power of love (8:6–7) and discusses with her friends the future of her little sister, who will soon be old enough for courtship (8:8–10). The bride likens her own body to a vineyard and Solomon to the owner of the vineyard (8:11–12). The Song ends with the voice of the bridegroom as he and his party approach the home of the bride at night to take her to the wedding:

> O you who dwell in the gardens,
>> my companions are listening for your voice;
>> let me hear it. (8:13, RSV)

And the bride responds:

> Make haste, my beloved,
>> and be like a gazelle

or a young stag
    upon the mountains of spices. (8:14, RSV)

In other words, "Here I am! Hurry up, and come get me!"
The setting for this would be the ancient Israelite wedding,
which would begin with a procession of the bridegroom
and his party to the home of the bride. There, the groom
and his groomsmen would collect the bride and bring her
to the house of the groom's father, where they would celebrate the wedding rites. So the Song of Songs ends with
the two main "voices"—those of the bride and the groom,
not yet married but about to be.

The oldest Jewish interpretations of the Song of Songs
understood it as an allegory of the romance between Israel
and God or Israel and the Messiah. Several features of the
Song make this kind of reading easy. For example, the
author compares the bride of the Song to many features
of the land of Israel and surrounding areas:

- the plain of Sharon in the north (2:1)
- the slopes of Gilead, east across the Jordan
  river (4:1, 6:5)
- the tower of David in Jerusalem (4:4)
- the territory of Lebanon in the north (4:11)
- the wealthy cities of Tirzah in the north and
  Jerusalem in the south (6:4)
- the pools of Heshbon in the land of Jordan to
  the east (7:4)
- the tower of Lebanon in the north near Damascus (7:4)
- Mt. Carmel on the western seacoast (7:5)

This makes sense if the bride of the Song in some sense *is* the land of Israel, which the prophet Isaiah describes as "married" to the Lord (Is 62:4).

Furthermore, the bride of the Song is constantly calling her fiancé/husband "my beloved" (twenty-six times in the book), which is spelled in Hebrew with the same letters as the name "David." Indeed, the name "David" means "Beloved One." This makes it easy to interpret the bride as calling out, "My David, my David!" "David" can mean the son or heir of David. For example, the prophets often call the Messiah "David," such as in Jeremiah 30:9, Ezekiel 34:23, and Hosea 3:5.

So when Jesus tells parables in which he compares himself to a royal bridegroom (Mt 22:2), he is drawing on this image of the royal bridegroom-messiah from the Song of Songs and elsewhere.

That doesn't mean the Song of Songs doesn't also speak about natural marriage. Indeed, the author could not use all the motifs of love, romance, and physical beauty in the Song of Songs as images of God's love for his people unless those things were good in themselves. No one can use things that are bad or evil as images of God's goodness! We can conclude that attraction, romance, marriage, and physical beauty are good things; indeed, they are gifts of God. More than just good, these things can actually be holy. For example, the bride describes the body of her groom as follows:

> His cheeks are like beds of spices,
>> mounds of sweet-smelling herbs.
> His lips are lilies,
>> dripping liquid myrrh.

His arms are rods of gold,
    set with jewels.
His body is polished ivory,
    bedecked with sapphires.
His legs are alabaster columns,
    set on bases of gold.
His appearance is like Lebanon,
    choice as the cedars. (Sg 5:13-15, ESV)

This is the imagery of the Temple in Jerusalem, which was adorned with precious materials. The priests burned sweet-smelling fragrances as incense on the altar or used them in the anointing oil. The bride is suggesting that the body of her beloved is a temple. That reminds us of Adam, whose body seems to be a temple (Gn 2:21) and of Jesus when he speaks of his body as a temple (Jn 2:19-21).

On the other hand, Solomon the bridegroom describes his bride's body as a supernatural and perfect garden, that is, the Garden of Eden, which was the first sanctuary or temple in history:

A garden locked is my sister, my bride,
    a spring locked, a fountain sealed.
Your shoots are an orchard of pomegranates
    with all choicest fruits,
    henna with nard,
nard and saffron, calamus and cinnamon,
    with all trees of frankincense,
myrrh and aloes,
    with all choice spices—
a garden fountain, a well of living water,
    and flowing streams from Lebanon. (Sg 4:12-15,
        ESV)

The bride's body is holy, too. This reminds us of what St. Paul says about Christians: "Do you not know that your body is the temple of the Holy Spirit?" (1 Cor 6:19). The lesson St. Paul draws is that we should keep ourselves chaste before and after getting married. Christians' bodies are holy, temples of the Holy Spirit. Only a holy person, a priest, could enter the sacred Temple, and only when authorized to do so. Christians should take care who enters their bodies; it should only be one's spouse, who has been made holy and authorized to do so by the Sacrament of Matrimony.

Some people don't recognize the holiness of marriage in the Song of Songs. Because a number of the poems seem to describe the bride and groom as being very close physically, some wrongly say that the Song of Songs shows that it's OK for young people to act as if they are married, even if they aren't. But that is far from true. Several verses of the Song place a high value on saving intimacy for one's spouse alone. Solomon says of his bride:

> A garden locked is my sister, my bride,
>   a spring locked, a fountain sealed. (Sg 4:12, RSV)

This means she had never been intimate with anyone before marrying him.

In a similar way, in Song 8:9–10, the younger sister of the bride is encouraged to be a "wall" rather than a "door" until she is married, and the bride herself boasts of being a "wall" as she enters her marriage (see Song of Songs 8:10, NABRE). That means she hasn't been close to any other man as she will be with her husband. The Song of Songs is not about being careless with one's body; rather, it puts a high value on chastity both before and in marriage. *Chastity* means saving the gift of our body for our spouse alone. When we decide to get married, we give the gift of our body to our spouse, and since it has not been given and never will be given to anyone else, that gift becomes something very special. You and your spouse have a rare and precious bond. No one knows you as your spouse does. Likewise, you know your spouse in a way no one else has or ever will. That very special connection of *exclusive* love helps bond the two of you together very strongly.

In the end, we don't need to choose between reading the Song as about Christ and the Church or about Christian marriage. Both are true. We see this in Ephesians 5, where St. Paul describes the marriage of Christ and the Church and the marriages of Christians at the same time. In Christian marriage, we take on the roles of Christ and the Church. And the Church is Christ's body—indeed, Christ himself. So both husband and wife channel Jesus Christ, the perfect spouse, toward each other.

Time to draw Solomon and his bride.

First, here goes Solomon!

We have to think of something to make him distinctive.
Let's go with . . .

. . . a big crown.

This is Solomon's ludicrous crown. I always draw him
with this huge crown so you know it's Solomon. But the
huge crown also works in this instance as there is a refer-
ence to Solomon's wedding crown in the Song: "Go forth,
O daughters of Zion, and behold King Solomon, with the
crown with which his mother crowned him on the day of
his wedding, on the day of the gladness of his heart" (Sg
3:11). The crown is actually an important image that will
come back at Jesus's Passion. But for now, let's move on
and give Solomon a scepter, too.

This is an image from Psalm 45, the royal wedding psalm, which is closely related to the Song of Songs. Psalm 45 says to Solomon: "Your royal scepter is a scepter of equity" (v. 6, RSV). *Equity* means fairness, justice, and righteousness.

Now we need to sketch in Solomon's bride. We will draw her next to him, with a less ludicrous and much more stylish crown.

In the Song of Songs, the bride is heaped with a lot of jewelry. We could really go overboard on this, but we will keep it tasteful and just give her a necklace of silver coins, very fashionable back in the day.

Of course, the setting plays an important role in the Song of Songs. The two lovebirds are always spending time with each other in an orchard or a vineyard. For the orchard, we will sketch in an apple tree.

Apples and apple trees are mentioned several times in the Song: "As an apple tree among the trees of the wood, so is my beloved among young men. With great delight I sat in his shadow" (2:3). So we will put Solomon and his bride in the shadow of an apple tree. It also reminds us of the Tree of Life, because the garden where the loving couple relaxes is described as if it were the Garden of Eden.

For the vineyard, let's draw in some grapevines.

Fresh grapes didn't last long without refrigeration, so they were eaten as raisins. Both raisins and apples were symbols of love: "Sustain me with raisins, refresh me with apples; for I am sick with love" (2:5).

Here's the royal couple happy in love.

Grapes were also consumed as wine, which was another symbol of the joy of love. The bride tells Solomon, "Your love is better than wine" (1:2), and promises him, "I would

give you spiced wine to drink" (8:2). So in the hand of the
bride we will put a goblet of wine.

Here is our final picture of Solomon and his bride. On
the one hand, they resemble Adam and Eve in the Garden
of Eden. On the other hand, they are images of Jesus and
the Church. We've seen how the garden imagery harks
back to Eden, but apples and grapes are symbols of marital
love, especially grapes in the form of wine. This sets us
up to see the deeper meaning in certain New Testament
events, such as the wedding at Cana.

Seven

God and Israel in the Prophets

In an earlier chapter, we saw how God espoused himself to Israel at Mt. Sinai. The people of Israel weren't faithful to God for very long. After forty days they went back to a god like those of the Egyptians by worshipping the golden calf. In fact, Israel tended to run after other gods all the time, especially during the wilderness wanderings and the time of the judges.

There was a brief period of faithfulness to the Lord, their husband-God, during the reign of David and the early reign of Solomon, but things went downhill quickly after that. Solomon overtaxed the people to fund his grand projects. When his son Rehoboam refused to lower taxes, the ten northern tribes of Israel, who had already "married" themselves to David and his heirs (2 Sm 5:1–3), now "divorced" the son of David (1 Kgs 12:16). They "moved in" with Jeroboam, a nobleman from the tribe of Ephraim, whom they made their king. Jeroboam led the people into spiritual adultery by establishing the worship of calf-idols rather than the true worship of the Lord (1 Kgs 12:28–33).

This idolatry in northern Israel became worse over the centuries, and eventually Judah, the name for the kingdom of the two southern tribes who stayed faithful to the line of David, began to practice idolatry too. As a punishment, God sent the nation Assyria to conquer and exile most of the northern Israelites from their land in 722 BC (2 Kgs 17:2–41) and the Judeans from their land in 587 BC (2 Kgs 25:1–26).

So it seems that the marriage of God and Israel ended in divorce and disaster. By the end of the historical books of the Bible, almost all seems lost (2 Kgs 25). But that's not how Israel's prophets saw it. The prophets of Israel condemned the people in strong language for breaking their covenant with God, but they also saw a time when God would "remarry" them by giving them a new covenant.

For example, the prophet Isaiah speaks to the Israelites in exile:

> Fear not, for you will not be ashamed;
>> be not confounded, for you will not be disgraced;
> for you will forget the shame of your youth,
>> and the reproach of your widowhood you will
>> remember no more.
> For your Maker is your husband,
>> the LORD of hosts is his name;
> and the Holy One of Israel is your Redeemer,
>> the God of the whole earth he is called.
> For the LORD has called you,
>> like a wife deserted and grieved in spirit,
> like a wife of youth when she is cast off,
>> says your God.
> For a brief moment I deserted you,

> but with great compassion I will gather you.
> In overflowing anger for a moment
>> I hid my face from you,
> but with everlasting love I will have compassion on
>> you. (Is 54:4–8, ESV)

In a similar way, Jeremiah says of Israel:

> Surely, as a faithless wife leaves her husband,
>> so have you been faithless to me, O house of Israel,
> says the LORD. (Jer 3:20, RSV)

And yet, despite that, the prophet calls:

> Turn back, rebellious children—declares the LORD.
> Since I have espoused you,
> I will take you . . . and bring you to Zion. (Jer 3:14, JPS
>> [1985])

Ezekiel, for his part, devotes two long chapters (16 and 23) to detailed and graphic depictions of the marriage of God and Israel. He describes God marrying Israel at Sinai:

> When I passed by you again and saw you,
> behold, you were at the age for love,
> and I spread the corner of my garment over you
> and covered your nakedness;
> I made my vow to you and entered into a covenant
>> with you,
> declares the Lord GOD, and you became mine. (Ez 16:8,
>> ESV)

But Israel had a long history of unfaithfulness:

But confident in your beauty and fame, you were
    unfaithful:
you lavished your favors on every passerby. (Ez 16:15,
    JPS [1985], alt.)

Yet for all that, the Lord God is committed to bringing
Israel back to himself:

Yet I will remember my covenant with you
in the days of your youth, and I will establish with you
an everlasting covenant. (Ez 16:60, RSV)

But without a doubt, the prophet who has the most
beautiful description of God's restored marriage with
Israel is the minor prophet Hosea. He doesn't whitewash
what Israel has done: "She burned incense to [the divine
'masters'] and decked herself with her ring and jewelry,
and went after her lovers, and forgot me, says the LORD"
(Hos 2:13, RSV).[4] But in the future the Lord God will make
himself irresistible to Israel:

Therefore, behold, I will allure her . . .
    and speak tenderly to her.
And there I will give her her vineyards. . . .
And there she shall answer as in the days of her youth,
    as at the time when she came out of the land of
    Egypt.
And in that day, says the LORD, you will call me, "My
husband," and no longer will you call me, "My [Master]."
For I will remove the names of the [divine masters] from
her mouth, and they shall be mentioned by name no
more. And I will make for you a covenant on that day.
. . . And I will betroth you to me forever; I will betroth
you to me in righteousness and in justice, in steadfast

love, and in mercy. I will betroth you to me in faithfulness; and you shall know the LORD. (Hos 2:14–20, RSV,
alternate translation)

Hosea has the most intimate language of any prophet
when describing the new covenant that the Lord will make
with Israel one day. God will "allure" Israel and speak "tenderly" to her. Israel had committed spiritual adultery by
worshipping harsh and demanding foreign gods, that
were called "masters" (Hebrew *ba'alim*, "Baals"). But in the
future, Israel won't call their God "my Master" (Hebrew
ba'ali) but "my husband" (Hebrew *'ishi*). God will make a
marriage covenant with his people: "I will make for you a
covenant . . . and I will betroth you to me forever." God's
people will come to "know" him, as spouses "know" each
other in the marital embrace: "you shall know the LORD"
(Hos 2:20, RSV).

Hosea is the first of the twelve minor prophets (the
prophets who authored the Old Testament books Hosea
through Malachi). The other minor prophets also speak
of Israel's unfaithfulness and the new covenant that God
will bring one day. The last of these prophets, Malachi,
rebukes the men of Judah for divorcing their wives in order
to marry foreign women, and he declares: "Let none be
faithless to the wife of his youth. 'For I hate divorce, says
the LORD the God of Israel'" (Mal 2:15–16). So the first
minor prophet insists that the Lord will remarry Israel,
and the last assures Israel that God hates divorce. The
combined message is that God will come back for Israel
one day and never let her go again! That's the way God
is. His greatest attribute is his *hesed*, a Hebrew word that
means "covenant love and faithfulness." It's the kind of

faithful love that spouses have for one another. St. John says "God is love," but this "love" (Greek *agapē*) is not merely brotherly love (Greek *philos*) or passing erotic love (Greek *eros*) but *faithful, covenantal love*—a love that is constant, undergoes suffering, and never gives up. That's also the love Christian spouses have toward each other, because we are called to live in imitation of God.

When God comes back to marry Israel again, some prophets predicted a great feast. This is how Isaiah describes it: "On this mountain the LORD of hosts will make for all peoples a feast of fat things, a feast of wine on the lees, of fat things full of marrow, of wine on the lees well refined" (Is 25:6, RSV). So when God returns to "marry" his people, it would be like a wedding banquet with plenty of wine.

Again, in another place Isaiah says:

> Ho, every one who thirsts,
>   come to the waters;
> and he who has no money,
>   come, buy and eat!
> Come, buy wine and milk
>   without money and without price. . . .
> Hearken diligently to me, and eat what is good,
>   and delight yourselves in fatness.
> Incline your ear, and come to me; . . .
> and I will make with you an everlasting covenant,
>   my steadfast, sure love [*hesed*] for David. (Is 55:1–3,
>   RSV)

Isaiah pictures God calling out to all the poor of the earth, people who are so poor that they have no money to buy food and drink. God invites all these poor people to a free banquet, a wedding banquet that will usher them into a covenant with him—the same loving covenant that David enjoyed. This is one of the texts that we read at the Easter Vigil every year, because it so clearly points forward to the Eucharist, the free banquet that is our "wedding supper" with the Lamb of God. Together, these prophecies help us understand why Jesus tells so many parables of the kingdom that involve weddings and feasting!

Time to draw. Again, this relationship between God and Israel is challenging to sketch. But we will take some ideas from our earlier chapter about Moses and Sinai.

We must have a mountain. In this case, it is Zion, the mountain of Jerusalem. Most of the prophets prophesied from Jerusalem and predicted that God would return there.

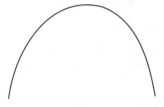

Next, we need our prophet. The way that we know it is a prophet is that he has a big mouth.

The prophets had big mouths; they ran them a lot and got themselves in trouble. But that's another story. Here, our prophet has one hand open, appealing to the people, and another hand making a point.

The third element of our sketch is going to be the Temple. We haven't discussed this yet, but the Temple played an important role in the prophet's picture of God's marriage with Israel. The Temple was what the old poets called a "trysting place," a place where a couple in love would go to be alone. The Temple was where God would meet his people as a bridegroom meets his bride.

God is the groom in this marriage, but it's hard to draw God. It was even forbidden in the Old Testament. But God often revealed his presence as a cloud of glory, as in the wilderness of Exodus. So we will draw the glory cloud of God coming down on the Temple, the "trysting place."

Now for the people. Here we will sketch in the same "crowd" of Israelites that we used at Sinai.

But they are the bridal people of God, so we give them veils and bouquets.

And there we go. The bridal people of God are gathered at the trysting place, the Temple, to join their bridegroom-God for a wedding banquet on Mt. Zion.

This is what the prophets foresaw and what Jesus came to fulfill.

Eight

Jesus the Bridegroom

The Gospel of John

By the time we get to the New Testament and the life-time of Jesus, the people of Israel had been waiting for their God to come back and "marry" them again for centuries, and expectations were at a fever pitch. The people of Judah—the southern kingdom that never "divorced" the son of David as their king—lost their land and kingdom and were exiled to Babylon back in the 500s BC. Babylon fell to the Persians, and the Persians had let the Jews go back to their homeland to rebuild Jerusalem and its Temple, but no son of David was put back on the throne. The people of Judah suffered under Persian rule (537–333 BC) and then under the Greek rule of Alexander the Great and his successors (333–166 BC). They briefly gained their independence (166–66 BC) only to lose it again to the Romans, who eventually put a pro-Roman king named Herod over them to keep them under control (37–4 BC).

The prophet Daniel had predicted an era of roughly five hundred years from the time of the rebuilding of

Jerusalem until the coming of the Messiah (Dn 9:25–27). It was hard to calculate these things in ancient times. Still, by the time of Jesus's birth, most people realized that Daniel's five hundred years were close to being over, so there were great expectations that God was about to do something for his people.

And he did. God sent his angel to a young woman of the line of David, Mary, to announce that she would conceive and give birth to Israel's Messiah. This Messiah was marked out as the bridegroom of Israel from his childhood. Wise men from the East arrived, bearing gifts of gold, frankincense, and myrrh. The last king of Israel to attract wise men from the East was Solomon (1 Kgs 4:30, 34), the hero of the Song of Songs. And the gifts of the wise men recall Solomon's splendor (Mt 2:11). Solomon had more gold than anyone (1 Kgs 10:14–23), and frankincense and myrrh are mentioned together in the Old Testament only in the Song of Songs (3:6; 4:6, 14), where they are romantic fragrances on the bodies of Solomon and his bride. The gifts of the Magi mark the child Jesus as the promised bridegroom-king!

Of the four gospels, John shows Jesus as the bridegroom most clearly. Jesus's first miracle in the Gospel of John is to change about 180 gallons of water into the finest wine for a wedding in Cana (Jn 2:1–11). The key to understanding this miracle is to ask, Whose job did Jesus do at this wedding? We might miss the point because in modern weddings, the father of the bride customarily pays for the reception and all its food and drink. But in Jesus's day, it was the responsibility of the *bridegroom* to provide wine for the wedding feast (Jn 2:9–10). So Jesus did the job of the bridegroom! Let's ask another question: Did he do it well or poorly? One hundred eighty gallons of the finest French Cabernet? I would say he did it well. In fact, I'm sure that after the wedding at Cana, Jesus started getting invitations from every engaged couple in Galilee!

Cana reveals Jesus as the greatest bridegroom ever, one who can do what a bridegroom is supposed to in a spectacular, supernatural way. The abundance of wine he makes is a sign of the abundance of God's grace that he brings (Jn 1:16). Jesus can give us, his bridal people, as much of God's grace as we can possibly "drink" (Jn 4:14).

In case we don't realize at Cana that Jesus is the great bridegroom, John the Baptist makes the point absolutely clear in the following chapter, where he calls Jesus the bridegroom outright. When asked about his identity, John says of himself: "You yourselves bear me witness, that I said, I am not the Christ, but I have been sent before him. He who has the bride is the bridegroom; the friend of the bridegroom, who stands and hears him, rejoices greatly at the bridegroom's voice; therefore this joy of mine is now full" (Jn 3:28–29).

Jesus is the bridegroom, and the bride is the people of God. John likens himself to the "friend of the bridegroom"—in our culture, the best man. Jesus is the bridegroom both as man and as God. As man, he is the heir of David, the original bridegroom-king of Israel (2 Sm 5:1–3). As God, he is Israel's husband, returned to woo her back (Hos 2:14–23).

In fact, almost immediately after John the Baptist's declaration that Jesus is the bridegroom, we have a courtship scene in the Gospel of John. In John 4, Jesus fulfills the prophecies of Hosea by going to the descendants of northern Israel and "speaking tenderly" to them (Hos 2:14).

Jesus decides to travel through Samaria (Jn 4:1–5) and about noon comes to a town called Sychar and sits down beside a well. Samaria was the region in the center of ancient Israel, made up of the territory of the northern tribes Ephraim and Manasseh. The Samaritans themselves were descendants of the poor farm workers from these and other northern tribes, who had intermarried with five Gentile ethnic groups brought in long ago by the invading Assyrians. The rest of the people of northern Israel had been exiled and scattered. This means the Samaritans were the last visible remnant of the northern tribes of Israel.

When Jesus sits down by the well, we know a woman is going to show up, because that's what always happens in the Bible when a man comes to a well. In Genesis 24,

Abraham's servant is out looking for a wife for Isaac. He comes to a well and meets Rebekah, who later becomes Isaac's bride. In Genesis 29, Jacob is traveling in the same area and comes to a well where he meets Rachel, and it is love at first sight. Later, in Exodus 2, Moses is fleeing Egypt and comes to the land of Midian, where he stops at a well and meets Zipporah, who later becomes his wife. So wells are the biblical place of courtship. Remember this sketch?

Our expectations are not disappointed, because no sooner does Jesus sit down than a woman from Sychar shows up to draw from the well. Jesus asks her for a drink (Jn 4:7). That's interesting, because a request for a drink was the divinely arranged pick-up line that Abraham's servant negotiated with God back in Genesis 24.

So when Jesus asks the woman of Samaria for a drink, our curiosity is piqued. Will she respond generously, like Rebekah? Actually, no. "How is it that you, a Jew, ask a drink of me, a woman of Samaria?" she asks Jesus (Jn 4:9). We now know that we are not just going to get a repeat of earlier biblical events. The conversation that follows is a kind of spiritual courtship, where Jesus tries to tell the woman about the gift of the Holy Spirit, but she keeps misunderstanding him as speaking about natural water

(vv. 10–15). Then the topic shifts to her marital status, and Jesus announces that he knows she has had five different husbands and is now living with a man she's not married to (vv. 16–18). The woman's personal life is a striking picture of the history of her people the Samaritans, who had intermarried with five different nations and worshipped their gods (2 Kgs 17:33–41). Eventually they returned to worshipping the Lord God alone, but they still did not worship him according to the covenant. They worshipped on Mt. Gerizim in Manasseh, whereas the covenant with David declared Jerusalem in Judah as the proper place of worship.

The conversation between Jesus and the woman now takes a theological turn (vv. 19–24). When the woman expresses hope in the coming of the Messiah, Jesus reveals himself as that hoped-for Savior (v. 26). Dumbfounded, the woman walks back into town and invites the whole village to come out and meet this amazing man she just encountered at the well (vv. 27–28). They do, and after two days of conversation with Jesus, they come to believe in him. Jesus has spiritually wooed these descendants of Israel back to himself, just as Hosea had said: "I will allure her . . . and speak tenderly to her. . . . And there she shall answer as in the days of her youth. . . . And in that day, says the LORD, you will call me, 'My husband' and no longer will you call me, 'My [Master.]' . . . And I will betroth you to me forever . . . and you shall know the LORD" (Hos 2:14–20, RSV, alternate translation).

But the real climax of Jesus's mission as the bridegroom comes later in the Gospel of John, as he approaches his Passion.

John's Passion Week account begins with the anointing
at the supper in Bethany. Mary, Lazarus's sister, brings a jar
of pure nard and anoints Jesus's feet as he reclines at the
meal. This recalls a line from the Song of Songs:

> While the king was on his couch,
>   my nard gave forth its fragrance. (Sg 1:12)

John even mentions that "the house was filled with the fragrance of the ointment" (Jn 12:3). Significantly, nard is only
found in the Old Testament in the Song of Songs, where
it is a romantic fragrance (1:12, 4:13–14). But Jesus insists
that this romantic luxury should be kept for his death:
"Let her keep [the rest of] it for the day of my burial" (Jn
12:7). That's a very provocative thing to say: What could
possibly be romantic about a funeral?

Yet when we fast-forward to Jesus's Passion in John,
we find many nuptial motifs. First, Jesus is crowned with
thorns, which calls to mind the wedding crown of the
royal son of David: "Go forth, O daughters of Zion, and
behold King Solomon, with the crown with which his
mother crowned him on the day of his wedding, on the
day of the gladness of his heart" (Sg 3:11). Some scholars
think this may have been a crown of flowers and vines,
made for the occasion of the royal wedding. By contrast,
what fine "foliage" was used to crown our bridegroom-
king, Jesus!

As we draw closer to the Cross, the soldiers remove
Jesus's clothing, as a bridegroom undresses to enter the
wedding chamber (Jn 19:23–24). Jesus, looking down from
the Cross, sees his own mother and the apostle John stand-
ing nearby. "Woman, behold, your son!" he says, and to
John, "Behold, your mother!" (Jn 19:26–27). When in real

life is it ever necessary to tell a woman that she has a son or
to introduce a mother and a son to each other? Only in the
birthing chamber, when a midwife cleans and clothes the
newborn child and then brings him back to his mother,
announcing, "Look! You have a son!" and cooing to the
boy, "Look, this is your mama!" Some spiritual authors
have seen here a kind of spiritual birth of the apostle John
and have described him as the first son of the Church, the
first offspring of the fruitful love of the New Adam (Jesus)
and the New Eve (Mary).

Not long after, Jesus says from the Cross, "I thirst" (Jn
19:28). This calls to mind the only other place in this gospel where he was thirsty, at the well at Sychar. There, he
also asked for a drink (Jn 4:7). St. Teresa of Calcutta saw
what this request was all about. She said, "He thirsts for
our love!" and had "I thirst" written near the tabernacles
in all the homes of her spiritual daughters. St. Teresa was
right; these words from Jesus are a request for our love, for
us to enter into a spousal relationship with him.

When we, God's bridal people, were thirsty at Cana,
Jesus gave us 180 gallons of the finest wine. But when he,
the bridegroom, is thirsty on the Cross, we give him nothing more than a sponge soaked in wine vinegar, held up
on a hyssop branch (Jn 19:29). It's not much of a response
of love, but Jesus accepts it and speaks his last words from
the Cross, "It is consummated" (Jn 19:30, Douay-Rheims).
When we use that older translation, we hear the connota-
tions of the completion of marriage, and indeed, the words
in the original language of the Gospel of John, Greek, can
carry this meaning.

The soldiers pierce the side of Jesus to ensure his death,
and out flows a stream of blood and water. St. Augustine

saw marital imagery in this event, whereas other church
fathers emphasized the parallel with Adam. As Eve came
forth from the opened side of Adam, so the Church comes
forth from the wounded side of Christ. The first readers
of John, however, would have thought first of the Temple.
During Passover, an enormous stream of blood and water
flowed from the Temple. Thousands of lambs were slaugh-
tered in the courtyard, and all their blood was washed
from the Temple with buckets of water down drains that
flowed to a pipe in the side of the Temple Mount. From
there, it gushed down the hillside into the Kidron brook.
It is a sign that Jesus's body is the true Temple, as John
had said earlier: "He spoke of the temple of his body" (Jn
2:21). That, in turn, connects back to Adam, for as we have
seen, the word used for the rib taken from his side refers
to a sacred beam or post used to support the tabernacle
or Temple (Gn 2:21).

Joseph of Arimathea and Nicodemus take Jesus's body
down from the Cross (Jn 19:38-39). Nicodemus brings
an enormous amount of myrrh and aloes—a hundred
pounds—to anoint the body (v. 39). This would have cost
a fortune. Myrrh and aloes are only mentioned together
in the Old Testament in strongly romantic contexts, such
as in the royal wedding psalm (Ps 45:8) and the Song of
Songs (Sg 4:14; cf. Prv 7:17). They were romantic fragrances
in ancient times, associated with the marriages of the very
wealthy. Jesus goes to his grave with fragrances fit for a
royal wedding.

Adam's "mother" was the earth herself (Gn 2:7), and
in the rest of John's Passion account we see more con-
nections between Adam and Jesus. Jesus is laid "in a new
tomb where no one had ever been laid" (Jn 19:41)—in other

words, a virginal tomb. How appropriate! He took flesh
from the virginal womb of his mother; then his flesh is laid
in the virginal tomb, the "womb" of Mother Earth. At least
half a dozen passages of scripture compare the mother's
womb with the grave or the earth:

> Naked I came from my mother's womb, and naked
> shall I return. (Jb 1:21)
> As he came from his mother's womb he shall go again,
> naked as he came. (Eccl 5:15)
> You knitted me together in my mother's womb. . . . I
> was . . . made in secret, intricately wrought in
> the depths of the earth. (Ps 139:13, 15)
> My mother would have been my grave, and her womb
> for ever great. (Jer 20:17)
> A heavy yoke is upon the sons of Adam . . . till the day
> they return to the mother of all. (Sir 40:1)

The womb of the Blessed Virgin gave birth to Jesus
on Christmas; the virginal tomb rebirths him at Easter.
Notably, *Nicodemus* places Jesus's body in the virginal
tomb. Earlier in the gospel, this same Nicodemus had
asked Jesus, "How can a man be born when he is old?
Can he enter a second time into his mother's womb and
be born?" (Jn 3:4). Yes, Nicodemus, each of us will enter
a second time into the womb of Mother Earth! But if we
have been baptized—the new birth of water and the Spirit
(Jn 3:5)—we will share Jesus's second birth from the grave,
when he comes again.

The whole drama of Jesus's Passion is the story of the
bridegroom giving his body to and for his bride. In his
death, Jesus gave us his body so that we could be saved for
eternal life. And every time we celebrate Mass, that gift of

his body is renewed. At Mass, he thirsts for our love, even as he satisfies our thirst for God's grace. And we should return his love to him, satisfying his thirst as he satisfies ours. Because of this, the Mass is called "the wedding feast of the Lamb."

It's time to gather this all together in a drawing. We need to start, of course, with the hill of Calvary.

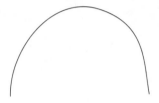

On top of Calvary, we sketch in Our Lord, the bride-groom. He hangs on a tree. A tree of death. But actually, he is transforming it into the true Tree of Life, which will bear the fruit of his Body and Blood, the food of eternal life.

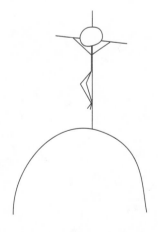

Now we put in the wounded side of Christ, gushing with blood and water, reminding us of the opened side of Adam, from which Eve was born.

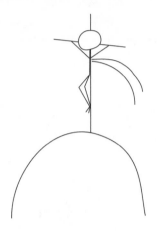

Next, we draw in the New Eve, Mary.

The true bride in this picture is the Church. But since earliest times, the fathers saw Mary, Virgin and Mother, as a sign of the whole Church. So we will let the Blessed Mother serve as the icon of the Church here.

Next, we add John, the fruit of the spiritual love of the New Adam and New Eve, the first son of the Church. John is like each baptized Christian, who has God as Father and Church as mother.

Finally, we put in Jesus's tomb, the Holy Sepulchre, in the background. There is a mystical connection between the virgin tomb and the virgin's womb. Both are icons of the Church, the bride of Christ.

    This is the bridegroom giving his life for the bride. This is God's love, his *hesed*, on full display. In this event lies the deepest meaning of marriage, salvation history, and the human condition. If a picture is worth a thousand words, this picture is the Book of Love.

Nine

Christ and the Church

Paul's Letter to the Ephesians

The Gospel of John shows us Jesus as the great bride-groom, giving his body as an act of love to and for his bride, which is the Church. That sounds beautiful, but what does it mean practically, for Christian husbands and wives? That's a question St. Paul addresses directly in the fifth chapter of his letter to the Ephesians, in a passage many consider to be the most profound teaching on Christian marriage in the New Testament. But St. Paul builds on Jesus's own teaching about marriage, which is something we have not yet discussed.

Jesus gave two major teachings about marriage during his earthly ministry. Both were in response to questions about marriage, one from the Pharisees and one from the Sadducees. In Matthew 19:3 we read that some Pharisees came to Jesus and asked, "Is it lawful to divorce one's wife for any cause?" This was a debate raging among Jewish scholars. Some leading Pharisees held that only serious immorality was grounds for divorce, while others held that a man could divorce his wife for any reason at all.[5] But Jesus disagrees: "He answered, 'Have you not read that he who made them from the beginning made them male and female, and said, "For this reason a man shall leave his father and mother and be joined to his wife, and the two shall become one"? So they are no longer two but one. What therefore God has joined together, let no man put asunder'" (Mt 19:4–6).

Jesus here teaches that divorce is wrong. It is God who joins a man and woman together when they marry. That bond is sacred, and human beings should not break it. But if the marriage bond is sacred, why does the Old Testament have laws that allow divorce? The Pharisees are quick to point this out, asking, "Why then did Moses *command* one to give a certificate of divorce, and to put her away?" (Mt 19:7, emphasis added).

The Pharisees are referring to a well-known law, given in Deuteronomy 24:1–4, but they are misreading it in a significant way. Moses never *commands* anyone to give a certificate of divorce. The actual law of this passage is quite specific and complicated: if a man divorces his wife for "indecency" and she remarries another who divorces her just for dislike, her first husband may not remarry her (v. 1). One might rightly ask, "What's that all about?" Scholars have some detailed explanations, but for now let's stay focused on what's most important; Moses nowhere *commands* divorce, but sometimes his laws acknowledge that it happens. Jesus makes the proper distinction in his reply: "For your hardness of heart Moses allowed you to divorce your wives, but from the beginning it was not so" (Mt 19:8).

Here Jesus teaches that Moses's laws do not always represent God's highest ideals. Moses permitted some things because of Israel's "hardness of heart," that is, their stubbornness. He knew that Israelites were so used to divorce that it was impractical to outlaw it. Most lawmakers, both ancient and modern, do similar things. For example, it might be best for public health if no one smoked at all. However, smoking is deeply ingrained in our culture, and prohibiting it completely would spark an uproar. So the government permits it but also regulates it. So it was with Moses and divorce. But, as Jesus points out, divorce was not God's intention for man and woman when he created the world. The early chapters of Genesis, before the fall into sin, do not envision the possibility of divorce. Therefore, Jesus continues, "I say to you, whoever divorces his wife (unless the marriage is unlawful) and marries another commits adultery" (Mt 19:9, NABRE).[6]

Jesus teaches that a *lawful* marriage cannot be broken by human beings. Even if a legal court grants a divorce, it means nothing from God's perspective. If a person then remarries, it is adultery, because that person is still married to their first spouse (*CCC* 1650). Now, there are unlawful marriages. If a man and woman do not follow the proper procedure to marry, or attempt to marry under the wrong conditions, there is no marriage in God's eyes. The Catholic Church will sometimes declare that a man and woman were never married in the eyes of God; this is called a declaration of nullity, or more popularly "an annulment," but it is not the same thing as a divorce (*CCC* 1629).

Not just the Pharisees but even Jesus's own disciples find his teaching shocking. They say, "If such is the case of a man with his wife, it is better not to marry" (Mt 19:10, ESV). The prospect of being bound to a woman for life without possibility of divorce was so daunting that the disciples would prefer to remain single! Their instincts aren't *all* bad, though, because Jesus points out that single-ness is something to be desired: "Not all can accept [this] word, but only those to whom that is granted. Some are incapable of marriage because they were born so; some, because they were made so by others; some, because they have renounced marriage for the sake of the kingdom of heaven. Whoever can accept this ought to accept it" (Mt 19:11–12, NABRE).[7]

The strength to live a single life is a gift granted by God. Not everyone can manage it, but those that God strengthens should do so (1 Cor 7:7–9, 32–38). Jesus him-self embraced the single life, as did John the Baptist, the apostles Paul and John, and many Christians down through the ages. Intentional singleness, often called celi-bacy, is not a rejection of love and marriage. It is a direct spiritual marriage to Jesus. In Christian marriage, the spouses act as Jesus toward each other. Wives experience the love of Jesus through their husbands and vice versa. But in the celibate life, that relationship is direct. One seeks and experiences Jesus's love not through another person but from Jesus alone in prayer and the sacraments. Thus, all Christians are called to a "marriage" with Jesus.[8]

Now, after Jesus's positive remarks about renouncing marriage for the sake of the kingdom, one might get the wrong impression that he held a low view of married love and its fruit, children. In order to correct that misunder-standing, St. Matthew immediately tells another story about Jesus's ministry: "Then children were brought to him that he might lay his hands on them and pray. The disciples rebuked the people; but Jesus said, 'Let the children come to me, and do not hinder them; for to such belongs the kingdom of heaven.' And he laid his hands on them and went away" (Mt 19:13–15).

Jesus loves children, and he teaches that they have a natural closeness to God's kingdom. He desires that children come to him to experience salvation. His words "let the children come to me, and do not hinder them" can also be applied in a spiritual sense to Christian marriages. Christian couples should let the children come—that is, be open to life. They shouldn't hinder the coming of children by the use of unnatural means to prevent conception and birth (CCC 1652, 2366–2370). Children are loved by God.

The second major occasion on which Jesus taught about marriage was when challenged by the Pharisees' opponents, the Sadducees. The Sadducees, a wealthy elite who controlled the Temple and its profits, did not believe in eternal life or the resurrection from the dead. In their opinion, resurrection would cause unsolvable dilemmas, and to make their point, they approached Jesus with a question: "Teacher, Moses said, 'If a man dies, having no children, his brother must marry the widow, and raise up children for his brother.' Now there were seven brothers among us; the first married, and died, and having no children left his wife to his brother. So too the second and third, down to the seventh. After them all, the woman died. In the resurrection, therefore, to which of the seven will she be wife? For they all had her" (Mt 22:24–28).

The Sadducees thought there was no answer to this question, and that was precisely their point: Look at how ridiculous the idea of a resurrection is! It would create a mess no one could unscramble! But Jesus is less than impressed with their argument, answering them, "You are wrong, because you know neither the Scriptures nor the power of God. For in the resurrection they neither marry nor are given in marriage, but are like angels in heaven" (Mt 22:29–30).

From this we learn that the marriage bond lasts only for this life. The death of one of the spouses ends a marriage, as reflected in the traditional wedding vows: "Until death do us part" or "as long as we both shall live." Other religions hold that marriage continues into eternity, but Jesus teaches that in the life to come we are "like angels." Notice he does not say we *become* angels—this is a common misunderstanding, often depicted in books, cartoons, and movies. No, we become *like* angels—like them in the sense that we do not marry or raise families. Since death ends the marriage bond, a surviving spouse can remarry in the Church (see 1 Corinthians 7:39–40).

Having taken a look at Jesus's teaching on marriage, we can return to Ephesians to see how St. Paul builds on the Lord's foundation. There is good reason to think St. Paul wrote his letter to the church in Ephesus late in his career, when his understanding of the Gospel had become deep and mature. Although most ancient copies of this letter are addressed to the church in Ephesus, it is very general and universal in its tone—applicable to Christians and churches in many different circumstances.

A major theme of Ephesians is that the Church is the Body of Christ. As a result, there are at least three "marriages" in the reality of the Church. First, there is the marriage of God and humanity in Christ, where the two become one flesh in Christ's body (Eph 1:22–23). Second, there is the marriage of Jew and Gentile in the Church, where these two become one flesh, one body in Christ (Eph 2:11–22). Third, there is the marriage of a Christian man to a Christian woman; in other words, the marriages of believers that make up the fabric of the church in Ephesus and elsewhere. The marriages of believing men and women overcome the hostility between man and woman that originated with the fall of our first parents (Gn 3:16b). The Church is the way God "marries" or unites himself to all creation and overcomes all the divisions that separate humanity.

Since the Church is Christ's body, it is also the Temple (cf. Jn 2:21). So Ephesians mixes terms from both anatomy and architecture when describing the Church. For example, Paul reminds the Ephesian Christians that they are "members of the household of God, built on the foundation of the apostles and prophets, Christ Jesus himself being the cornerstone, in whom the whole structure, being joined together, grows into a holy temple in the Lord" (Eph 2:19–21, ESV). "Foundation," "cornerstone," "structure," and "temple" are all terms from the building trades. Yet in another place, Paul encourages the people to "grow up in every way into him who is the head, into Christ, from whom the whole body, joined and knit together by every joint with which it is supplied, when each part is working properly, makes bodily growth and upbuilds itself in love" (4:15–16). "Head," "body," "joint," "part," and "growth" are all words a doctor might use in the exam room. This double role of the Church as both *body* and *temple* reminds us of many scripture texts, going all the way back to Genesis 2, where we noted that the word used for Adam's rib usually refers to a sacred beam or support in the sanctuary

(v. 21) and that God "built" Eve from it (v. 22, Douay-Rheims). This suggests that both Adam's and Eve's bodies were already sacred temples, dwelling places of the "breath of life," God's own Spirit (Gn 2:7; Jb 27:3).

After laying the foundation (no pun intended!) of the Church as God's Temple and the Body of Christ, St. Paul moves to practical instructions for Christians in Ephesians 4–6. He places great stress on unity and cooperation among Christians; although we have different roles and gifts, we need to remember that we are all part of one body, Christ (Eph 4:11–16). Just as a body has many different parts that cooperate for the good of all, so Christians must cooperate as a body (Eph 4:16). Sin gets in the way of that harmony and cooperation, so Paul spends several verses warning about various kinds of sins that damage the Church (Eph 4:17–5:20). Getting along harmoniously requires us to put others before ourselves, and Paul uses a special Greek word for this others-first attitude: *hupotassomai* (HOOP-oh-TASS-oh-my). Literally, it means to "place yourself under" someone else. It is a general disposition that all Christians should have, and Paul uses it to sum up the Christian lifestyle: "[Place yourselves under] one another out of reverence for Christ" (Eph 5:21). Translations usually read "be subject to one another" (RSV) or "be subordinate to one another" (NABRE), but these words can have a negative connotation in English that Paul did not intend.

This Christian lifestyle of putting others first has a special application to Christian marriage. Here I'll use a modern translation, but substitute the literal meaning of *hupotassomai* where it occurs: "Wives should [place themselves under] their husbands as to the Lord. For the husband is head of his wife just as Christ is head of the church, he himself the savior of the body. As the church [places herself under] Christ, so wives should [place themselves under] their husbands in everything" (Eph 5:22–24, NABRE, translation adjusted).

Now, in calling him "head," Paul assigns a leadership role to the husband in the home. But men ought not to let this role "go to their head," so to speak, because we need to remember Jesus's very strong teaching on how to lead within the Church. When the apostles were arguing about who was greatest at the Last Supper, Jesus told them, "The kings of the Gentiles lord it over them and those in authority over them are addressed as 'Benefactors'; but among you it shall not be so. Rather, let the greatest among you be as the youngest, and the leader as the servant. For who is greater: the one seated at table or the one who serves? Is it not the one seated at table? I am among you as the one who serves" (Lk 22:25–27, NABRE).

In this passage, Jesus contrasts two concepts of leadership. The first is what I call the "demonic view," because it's the view of leadership held by Satan and all who follow him:

In this view, service flows up from those led to the leader himself. According to tradition, Satan was offended by the idea that he, the greatest of the angels, would be required to serve human beings. That didn't fit Satan's view of reality; he felt the lesser should serve the greater. So he rebelled.

Jesus's view of leadership is quite different. In Jesus's view, service flows from the leader to those who are led. The leader performs a service for everyone else—organizing, encouraging, guiding, but most of all, taking responsibility for the common good.

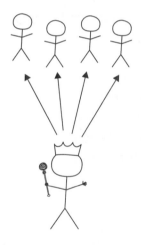

Not long ago I read a book on leadership by a couple of retired soldiers who had been part of a very famous and elite commando unit. I was surprised by their main principle of leadership, which they learned in combat but applied to all aspects of life: a leader takes 100 percent responsibility when things go wrong, and when things go right, he gives all credit to his team. These tough-as-nails soldiers insisted this was not just *a* way to lead but the *only* way that leads to success for everyone, regardless of the situation. I was struck by how similar this principle is to Jesus's teaching and example. Jesus took 100 percent responsibility for our sins and wrongdoings on the Cross (1 Pt 2:24). And every time we make even a small amount of progress in holiness, Jesus takes note of it and blesses it so that we can merit heaven (Mt 10:42). In this way, Jesus provides the best possible example of leadership. At the Last Supper, Jesus was warning the apostles, "If you think being a leader is all about you, you are thinking like a pagan!" For Jesus, leadership is service. A leader accepts responsibility for the well-being of others.

Getting back to Ephesians 5 and Paul's teaching on marriage, there are some other things we should note. St. Paul says, "Wives should place themselves under their husbands," usually translated something like, "Wives, be subject to your husbands" (Eph 5:21). Notice that St. Paul encourages wives to act this way of their own free will. He does not say, for example, "Husbands, place your wives under yourselves." In fact, there is no passage in the Old or the New Testament that tells husbands to make their wives do anything. A wife's behavior is her own free choice, and St. Paul respects that. The respect a wife shows to her husband is an act of love, and love cannot be coerced. It must be voluntary. It must always be freely chosen.

St. Paul continues, "As the church places herself under Christ, so let wives also place themselves under their husbands *in everything*" (Eph 5:24, emphasis added). St. Paul rightly says "in everything" because he is stressing the total self-gift of marriage. A wife gives herself totally to her husband, just as the husband gives himself totally to his wife. In a moment, we will look at the husband's role of self-giving. But for now, let's recognize that when Paul says "in everything," he assumes the husband is following the example of Christ. Obviously, we should never follow anyone into sin, not even our spouse. That includes sins against ourselves. As St. Peter says elsewhere, "We must obey God rather than men" (Acts 5:29).

Now let's look at what St. Paul says to husbands. I think you will agree that he places some very strong expectations on them: "Husbands, love your wives, as Christ loved the church and gave himself up for her, that he might sanctify her, having cleansed her by the washing of water with the word, that he might present the church to himself in splendor, without spot or wrinkle or any such thing, that she might be holy and without blemish" (Eph 5:25–27, RSV).

St. Paul calls on husbands to love their wives in a special way: "as Christ loved the church and gave himself up for her" (v. 25). This phrase, "gave himself up," is an Old Testament expression that refers to a person being handed over to his enemies (Is 42:24). This is the model of love that Jesus sets for husbands—to love their wives even to the point of death. But St. Paul goes on and describes Jesus as "sanctifying," "cleansing," and "washing" the Church so that she might be "holy and without blemish." Here, St. Paul is drawing on a famous parable about the marriage of the Lord and Israel from the prophet Ezekiel (Ez 16:8–14). The point is that husbands should be concerned about the spiritual welfare of their wives, doing whatever they can to help them grow in holiness. After all, the most loving thing husbands can do for their wives is to help them get to heaven.

St. Paul continues: "In the same way husbands should love their wives as their own bodies. He who loves his wife loves himself. For no one ever hated his own flesh, but nourishes and cherishes it, just as Christ does the church, because we are members of his body" (Eph 5:28–30, ESV). Everyone knows that, after the command to love God, the second most important commandment is to "love your neighbor as yourself" (Lv 19:18). Here, St. Paul applies that commandment to husbands and wives. Who is a closer "neighbor" than one's spouse? So "he who loves his wife loves himself" (Eph 5:28b).

Christ sets an example for husbands by "nourishing" and "cherishing" the Church, his body (v. 29). The words St. Paul uses here are touching. His word for "nourish" is related to the Greek verb for a mother nursing her baby. The word for "cherish" originally meant "to warm" and referred to a mother bird keeping her eggs and chicks warm in the nest. St. Paul describes a husband's love for his wife with great tenderness, with motherly terms. For this is how *Christ* loves *us*, we who are the Church, his body and bride.

St. Paul brings his discussion of marriage to a close by quoting the famous verse that has stood in the background of everything he has said: "'Therefore a man shall leave his father and mother and hold fast to his wife, and the two shall become one flesh' [Gn 2:24]. This mystery is profound, and I am saying that it refers to Christ and the church. However, let each one of you love his wife as himself, and let the wife see that she respects her husband" (Eph 5:31–33, ESV).

Genesis says a man shall "hold fast" to his wife. According to older translations, a man should "cleave" to his wife. The Hebrew word for "hold fast" or "cleave" is very strong. It means "get stuck to," like something glued together that can't be removed. St. Paul says the image of this perfect, "unremovable," one-flesh union in Genesis 2:24 is actually Christ and the Church. It's not that true marriage is between a man and a woman, and the bond between Christ and the Church is kind of like it. No, it's the reverse. True marriage is the bond between Christ and the Church, and marriage between a man and a woman is kind of like it. Wow! That's hard to comprehend. We have to let it soak in. That's why St. Paul says, "this mystery is profound." The Greek word for "mystery" can also be translated "sacrament."

St. Paul's final comment sums up how husbands and wives should treat one another. I'll give my own translation: "Let every single one of you love his wife as himself, and let the wife respect her husband" (v. 33). Both are called to show the others-first attitude expressed by the word *hupotassomai*, "putting yourself under." But they do so in different ways, because men and women are different. That's a good thing! As the French say, *viva la différence!* The way a husband puts his wife first and "places himself under" is by loving her as his own self, even to the point of laying down his life for her. And the way a wife puts her husband first is by showing him respect as the head of the family.

Even the most pleasant and beautiful human activities need some organization, some leadership. Take dancing, for example. Dancing is fun. Dancing is enjoyable. People do it for its own sake, for the pleasure of it. Dancing takes place between partners who are equals, but still, someone needs to lead. And in traditional ballroom dance, that's the guy. If he's a good dancer, his leading is gentle and barely noticeable—only so much as is necessary for the couple to keep in time and pull off their moves together. If he can't lead in such a way that his partner enjoys herself, he'll end up spending a lot of time alone by the punch bowl!

Marriage is like dancing. God intends it to be a wonderful cooperation between two equal partners who complement each other and work together, with just enough leadership to stay organized and keep moving forward in harmony. Jesus is the perfect example of the husband who leads in a gentle and self-giving way, and the saints are the image of the bride who follows Christ closely in the incredible dance of love the Father has choreographed.

To sketch some key concepts from this chapter, let's begin with the joined hands of a married couple.

Those lines are going to form the heart of this little icon of marriage because the union of the two is the central truth and reality of matrimony.

Next, drawing out from the joined hands, we sketch in
the groom and the bride.

Now we are going to try something unlike any other
sketch we've done before, in this book or my others. Those
joined hands of the bride and groom are going to form the
outstretched arms of Christ. And around the hands we are
going to draw the heart of Christ, the Sacred Heart.

This reminds us that what binds Christian spouses
together is not just their love, but first and foremost the
love of Jesus. Human love has its limits. For couples to
weather the storms of life, with all the threats to their marriage bond, they are going to need divine love that flows
from the heart of Jesus.

Next, let's sketch in the Cross.

This reminds us that, like all the other sacraments, Matrimony flows from the Cross and participates in the Cross. Both spouses experience the Cross in marriage. The husband offers his life even to death for the sake of his wife, as Christ gave himself for the sake of the Church on the Cross. Likewise, the wife gives her whole self to her husband, just as Jesus gave his whole self to the Father on the Cross. What flows from these acts of sacrifice is new life, just as Jesus's body flowed with blood and water on Calvary.

Finally, in the background we add the joined rings that are a traditional symbol of marriage. Just as two joined metal rings cannot be separated, so a true marriage is indissoluble. It becomes a participation in the unbreakable love of Christ, poured out for us on the Cross.

Ten

The Lamb and the New Jerusalem

The Book of Revelation

Even people who otherwise know very little about the Bible are often aware that its last book is the notorious book of Revelation. The fantastical images and supernatural plagues described in this book fascinate some people and turn others off. Debates rage about the interpretation of Revelation and what it says about the final judgment and the end of world history. Sadly, in the midst of those debates, people lose sight of the very strong marriage theme that runs through this final biblical book.

There is an allusion to marriage in Revelation's very name. The full name of the book is "The Revelation to St. John," or alternatively, "The Apocalypse of St. John." The words "revelation" and "apocalypse" mean the same thing. The first is Latin, the second Greek. Latin *revelatio* is a combination of two words: *re*, which means "back," and *velatio,* which means "veil." So *re-velatio* means "pulling back the veil." It is the same in Greek. The word *apo* means "off" and *calypsis* means "veil," so *apo-calypsis* means "taking off the veil." It's what happened at the wedding ceremony in ancient cultures when the bride entered the wedding chamber and took off her veil so that her husband could see her beauty for the first time in their life together as man and wife.

Let's give a little overview of the plot of the book of Revelation. When the book begins, St. John is on the island of Patmos, exiled for being a Christian leader. Patmos is a few miles off the coast of Ephesus in Asia Minor, an area that now makes up the country of Turkey. St. John is deep in prayer on a certain Sunday when the resurrected Jesus suddenly appears to him and commands him to write down letters to the churches in seven cities on the mainland. Each church is facing a different problem: there is the loveless church of Ephesus, the persecuted church of Smyrna, and the self-indulgent church of Pergamum. Thyatira is immoral, Sardis is spiritually dead, Philadelphia powerless, and Laodicea lukewarm. To each church, Jesus gives counsel, rebuke, and encouragement appropriate to the situation (Rv 2–3).

Then St. John is taken up into heaven and sees the heavenly liturgy, the reality of the angels and saints worshipping God (Rv 4–5). At every Mass, we take part in this heavenly worship through faith and the sacraments, but we can't see it. In Revelation, John tries to share with us what he experienced.

After taking it all in for a couple of chapters (Rv 4–5), John begins to see the earthly effects of the heavenly worship. Every time a heavenly worshipper performs a sacred action, plagues fall on earth against the enemies of God's people. First, seven seals are opened on seven sacred scrolls, pouring out seven plagues on the earth (chs. 6–7).

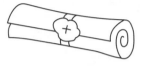

Then angels blow seven trumpets (chs. 8–11), releasing more plagues.

Finally, seven bowls are poured out, the final set of punishments (chs. 15–16).

At that point, judgment falls on one of the main villains of Revelation, the immoral woman named Babylon (Rv 17:5). She is the very opposite of a bride. Instead, she is a woman who doesn't love any man but shares herself with many for the sake of becoming wealthy. She is identified as "the great city which has dominion over the kings of the earth" (Rv 17:18). While at first this sounds like Rome, a stronger case can be made that the woman Babylon is the earthly city of Jerusalem. I can't present the whole argument here, although I have done so in another book.[9] But just to be brief: in Revelation 11:8, the "great city" is identified as the place where Jesus was crucified, so clearly Jerusalem. It is also called "Sodom" and "Egypt," two names the Old Testament prophets used for Jerusalem (Rv 11:8; Is 1:10; Jer 23:14; Am 4:10–11). The city has "dominion over the kings of the earth" (Rv 17:18) because such rule was promised to Jerusalem in the Old Testament (see Psalms 110:2, 48:2). The great wealth of the city in Revelation 18 reflects the fact that Jerusalem was one of the wealthiest, perhaps *the* wealthiest, city in the Roman Empire. And she was also the site of the martyrdom of the Old Testament prophets as well as the early Christian martyrs (Rv 18:24; Mt 23:32–38).

The immoral woman sits on a seven-headed dragon, whose heads symbolize hills (Rv 17:7–9). It was well-known that the city of Rome had seven hills, so the dragon is very likely the Roman Empire. The woman sits on this dragon, meaning she was supported by it (v. 9). This was true of the leadership class of the city of Jerusalem; the royalty descended from King Herod, as well as the Sadducees and Pharisees, stayed in power because they collaborated with the Romans, who collected the temple taxes on their behalf. Near the end of Revelation 17, the beast turns on the woman and "burn[s] her up with fire" (v. 16), which is exactly what happened in the years AD 66–70: the relationship between Rome and Jerusalem broke down, and the Romans came and burned Jerusalem to the ground, just as Jesus had predicted (Mt 24:2; Mk 13:2; Lk 19:44, 21:6).

The tale of the earthly Jerusalem is a tragic love story. In both the Old Testament (Ez 16:8–14) and the New

(Mt 23:37; Lk 13:34), God loved Jerusalem very much, as a bridegroom loves his bride, but Jerusalem was never faithful to the Lord. At last, she ends up destroyed, not by the Lord but by those she ran after and loved more than him. But this does not happen before Jesus builds a New Jerusalem around himself, a city made not of stones but of persons (1 Pt 2:5; Eph 2:19–22; Heb 12:22). Jesus's disciples are the true Jerusalem. What was special about Jerusalem was not its unique stones, soil, or location, but that the true Temple was there and the true worshippers of God lived there. As we saw in the chapter on the Gospel of John, Jesus has become the true Temple (Jn 2:21), and those gathered together to worship him are the true city, the New Jerusalem.

That's what we see in the book of Revelation. After the earthly Jerusalem has been tragically destroyed, we see "the holy city, new Jerusalem, coming down out of heaven from God, prepared as a bride adorned for her husband" (Rv 21:2). The old is replaced by the new, the unfaithful by the faithful. John continues: "I heard a loud voice from the throne saying, 'Behold, the dwelling of God is with men. He will dwell with them, and they shall be his people, and God himself will be with them; he will wipe away every tear from their eyes, and death shall be no more, neither shall there be mourning nor crying nor pain any more, for the former things have passed away'" (Rv 21:3–4, RSV).

A central feature of marriage is that the spouses live together and share their lives; in a similar way, now "the dwelling of God is with men." His love for his people is very tender: "He will wipe away every tear from their eyes." We are naturally protective of our eyes. If a stranger even reaches toward our face, we instinctively raise our arms to shield ourselves. Only people we trust very much are allowed to touch our face, even to "wipe away every tear." God is very close to us, like a spouse who has our complete trust.

John describes the bride, the New Jerusalem, with many other beautiful images. We learn that she has twelve foundations, and each one bears the name of an apostle (Rv 21:14). This helps us to identify her with the Church, which St. Paul says is "built upon the foundation of the apostles" (Eph 2:20). An angel measures the city and finds that it is a perfect cube: "its length and breadth and height are equal" (Rv 21:16).

The only other perfect cube in the Bible is the Holy of Holies, the heart of the Temple (1 Kgs 6:20). There was a Jewish tradition that, at the end of time, the holiness of the Temple would expand to fill the whole city of Jerusalem (see Zechariah 14:20–21). John sees the ultimate fulfillment of this tradition: the city of the New Jerusalem is not just one big Temple but one big *Holy of Holies*! The message here is that the Church is holy in every part, because God dwells in each one of her members. We are all "living stones" in God's Temple, as Peter says (1 Pt 2:5), and Paul insists "your body is a temple of the Holy Spirit" (1 Cor 6:19). Under Moses, God's presence was limited to the Holy of Holies, above the ark of the covenant, where Moses went to speak to God (Ex 25:22). But now God's presence is in every Christian, from the newly baptized infant to the pope himself. The entire Church is a Holy of Holies!

The end of Revelation has several other romantic marriage images. The New Jerusalem contains the Tree of Life and the River of Life—just like Eden, the garden that hosted the very first wedding, of Adam and Eve. All who are thirsty will have their thirst satisfied (21:6, 22:17), and thirst has been connected to romance ever since the courtship of Rebekah (Gn 24:14). At the end of the book, the spouses call back and forth to each other: "The Spirit and the Bride say, 'Come'" (Rv 22:17). The bridegroom responds, "I am coming soon," and John chimes in on behalf of the whole Church-bride, "Amen. Come, Lord Jesus!" (Rv 22:20). This reminds us of the ending of the Song of Songs, when the bridegroom shows up with his wedding party, looking for the bride: "My companions are listening for your voice; let me hear it," and she responds, "Make haste, my beloved, and be like a gazelle" (Sg 8:13–14). The Song of Songs speaks for God's people in the old covenant, calling for the bridegroom-messiah to make haste and come to them. Revelation speaks for the Church in the new covenant, calling for Jesus to come back soon. Both books are filled with the romance of God and his people.

We don't have to wait until the end of the world to experience the book of Revelation and the intimacy of God as spouse. The streets of gold of the New Jerusalem are often said to describe heaven, but at every Mass, heaven comes down to earth. Or better—earth is raised up to heaven. The Tree of Life and River of Life in the New Jerusalem are present already in the Eucharist and

Baptism. That's why at the center of each Mass, the priest proclaims, "Blessed are those who are called to the wedding feast of the Lamb!" One day we will see him face-to-face, but even now, when we exercise our faith, we can experience the closeness of Jesus the bridegroom every time we take his body into ours in the Eucharist.

Truly, the wedding at the end of Revelation is one of the most unusual images in all the Bible. First of all, the bride is a perfect cube:

We will give her a veil, at least.

And she has to have wings, because she is flying down out of heaven to meet her bridegroom.

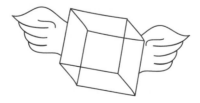

Her destination is the new Mt. Zion, which has the Tree of Life and the River of Life.

There, on the new Mt. Zion, is her bridegroom, the Lamb.

In Revelation 21:2, St. John describes the New Jerusalem descending to meet the Lamb.

When at last they meet, it is the wedding feast of the
Lamb, the final union of Christ and the Church, of God
and his people. This is the vision of wedded bliss that ends
the Bible.

Eleven

What Can We Learn?

We've covered a lot of ground in this book. We've traveled from the beginning of human history in the Garden of Eden to its end in the New Jerusalem. Through it all, we've seen how central marriage is to God's plan for the human race. One could even make the case that it is the central theme of the whole Bible.

A Review of Marriage through the Bible

Adam and Eve. We have seen how the marriage between Adam and Eve was the high point of the whole creation story; everything built up to it. This is because Adam and Eve were the images of God on the earth. Since God himself is a community of persons—in fact, two persons whose bond of love becomes a third—he made humanity in his image to rule his creation, and he made human beings like himself. Humans were not made to live as individual persons but to bond in love with another person and allow that love bond to become a third, a child. So marriage is a reflection of who God is. And when we humans live marriage well, we become more like God and shine as images of God within the world.

Of course, Adam and Eve broke their covenant with God, and that breech seriously damaged their marriage covenant as well. It is the beginning of a pattern that we see throughout the Bible and throughout human history: damage to humanity's relationship with God results in damage to marriage, too. The covenant of God and man is perfectly tuned with the covenant of man and woman. So when Adam and Eve rebel against God, it also introduces trouble in their relationship with each other. Now they will fight each other for control, the "battle of the sexes."

Noah and His Wife. As we followed the Bible story line, we saw other offenses against marriage spring up as the years passed. Lamech, a descendant of Cain, was the first to get the wicked idea of taking more than one wife, and this soon led to widespread polygamy, which in turn provoked the Flood. The Flood was a reboot of human history, resetting everyone and everything to monogamy; every man and beast that went on the ark was monogamous. But the reboot didn't last long, as Noah himself sinned by letting others see what only his wife should behold, and once again the human race grew apart from God.

Abraham and Sarah. We see God reaching out once more to humanity through Abraham and his family. Since Abraham's family was to be the source of salvation and blessing for the whole human race, it was important to keep the family healthy and holy, and that began with good marriages. Great effort was made to find suitable spouses for Isaac and Jacob, spouses who worshipped the same God, so the children would be raised in God's covenant. Sure, the patriarchs did not always marry well. Abraham foolishly listened to Sarah and took a second wife. Laban tricked Jacob into marrying two sisters, and they in turn pushed their maids on him. But the patriarchs themselves never wanted more than one wife. And God worked with them through the messes these extra marriages caused to build up the nation of Israel from Jacob's twelve sons.

God and Israel. It was that nation of Israel that God himself "married" in the book of Exodus, sending Moses like a best man to escort his bride Israel out of Egypt to the trysting place, Mt. Sinai. There God and Israel exchanged vows: "All that the LORD has spoken we will do" (Ex 24:7). But the honeymoon didn't last long, and forty days later the Israelites went back to good old-fashioned, foot-stomping, hand-raising Egyptian bull worship. This was spiritual adultery. But Moses pleaded and God forgave. In the aftermath, God revealed his true "name," or nature, to Moses: "The LORD, the LORD, a God merciful and gracious, slow to anger, and abounding in steadfast love [*hesed*] and faithfulness, keeping steadfast love [*hesed*] for thousands" (Ex 34:6–7, RSV). The only quality God mentions more than once when he describes himself is *hesed*.

This quality, translated above as "steadfast love," is hard to express in English. I would define it as "the love that covenant partners should have for one another, a loving faithfulness or faithful love—the love of spouses." Since ancient times scholars translated it with the word "mercy," giving rise to the tradition that God's greatest attribute is his mercy. True enough, but God's "mercy" is really his covenantal, spousal love. When later St. John the Apostle says, "God is love," he is building on the revelation

to Moses in Exodus 34:6–7, translating *hesed* with *agapē,*
the Greek word for the highest form of love—the love
between spouses and God's love for human beings. We
can agree with St. John that God is love, but this love is
not physical attraction or warm feelings but *hesed,* the
faithfulness of a covenant partner or spouse, a love "till
death do us part."

Boaz and Ruth. Israel didn't keep *hesed* with God—
that's the story of the Bible from Exodus through 1 Samuel—but there were some lights during these turbulent
times. We looked at one in particular, the romance of Ruth
and Boaz, who unwittingly lived out the romance of Jesus
and the Church in advance. These were two people who
practiced *hesed*—faithful love. Ruth showed faithfulness
to Naomi, Boaz showed faithfulness to his female in-laws,
and faithfulness brought the two of them together, to fall
in love with each other and raise a family that led to the
Messiah.

Solomon and His Bride. The ancestor of that Messiah would be their great-grandson David, who rose
through the ranks of Saul's army to become the greatest
king of Israel. He was a kind of bridegroom-king, because
the people of Israel came to him and said, "We are your
bone and flesh" (2 Sm 5:1). This statement of the people
reminds us of what Eve was to Adam. That bridegroom
character showed itself even more in David's son Solomon,
who became Israel's most famous bridegroom because of
the love songs composed about him. Solomon seemed
intent on marrying the whole world, one woman at a time!
With seven hundred wives, he definitely went about it the
wrong way, but the idea of a bridegroom for the whole
world goes back to Adam and points forward to Jesus.

Jesus the Bridegroom. After Solomon, the fortunes of Israel went downhill, but the great men who prophesied during this time of decline, such as Hosea, spoke often of God returning to re-wed his people. And that's what we see happening in the gospels, as Jesus in subtle and not-so-subtle ways shows himself to be the divine bridegroom returned to take bride-Israel to himself. We saw this in the parables of Matthew and especially in the Gospel of John, which begins with a wedding at Cana and ends with a "wedding" at the Cross, where Jesus the bridegroom gives his body for his bride the Church in the most mysterious marriage in all cosmic history.

Christ and the Church. St. Paul takes up that mystery of the marriage of Christ and the Church and holds it up as the model and example for all Christian married couples (Eph 5:20–30). Paul's words are profound and sometimes challenge the ideas of marriage in our contemporary society. But then, marriage in our society is a disaster, so we shouldn't be surprised to find that its notions are out of step with God's word. But Paul calls husbands and wives to take up the roles of Jesus and the Church respectively and become images of the marriage that is the source of salvation for the human race. Actually, since the Church is nothing other than Christ's body, Christ himself, we can say both husband and wife are called to become Jesus to each other, in complementary ways.

Living Marriage Today

That brings us to the present, and we can ask the question, So what? What does our tour of love and marriage through the Bible teach us about how we should live *now*, in the twenty-first century, as baptized disciples of Jesus and members of his holy Church? Let's draw some practical applications from our tour of the Bible.

From our study of the creation story and the marriage of Adam and Eve, we learn the beauty of *openness to life.* "Be fruitful and multiply" was the first blessing and command given to the human race, and this only comes about through marriage. Each new child is of infinite worth, because—unlike a car, boat, luxury home, or any other possession—they are made in the image of God. The love of the first two persons of the Trinity is always open to the third, and so the love of married persons should always be open to becoming a third.

From our look at Noah and the epic of the Flood, we learn the importance of *monogamy.* Rampant polygamy created the social chaos that brought on the Flood, and every man and animal saved through the ark was monogamous. The logic of monogamy is lifelong, because divorce and remarriage amount to serial polygamy—multiple spouses in a row rather than all at the same time. The logic of self-gift in marriage demands one-to-one equality, so each spouse gives himself or herself completely to the other, and no spouse is "shared" during their lifetime.

From our overview of the patriarchs, we see the value of *marrying within the community of faith.* Abraham spares no expense or effort to find a spouse for Isaac who worships the same God. If the true faith is to continue for even one more generation, it requires parents who marry within the faith. "Do not be unequally yoked," St. Paul exhorts us (2 Cor 6:14, ESV).

At the events at Mt. Sinai and God's betrothal with Israel, we observe the crucial roles of *fidelity* and *forgiveness.* The people of Israel failed to show fidelity, turning their back on their bridegroom-God after only forty days, doing damage to the relationship that could never be fully healed. God, however, showed himself faithful to Israel, even naming himself twice with the Hebrew word for faithful love: *hesed.* And that fidelity was expressed in *forgiveness.* I know of a wise priest who says the same thing at every wedding: "If you can't forgive, don't marry."

In the gloom and chaos of the time of the judges, the story of Ruth and Boaz shines like a candle in the darkness, showing us that *the health of society depends on marriage.* Every culture needs good leaders, but virtuous men and women do not drop from the sky. They are born and raised, and holy marriages are the greenhouses where virtuous leaders grow. It is difficult for children without a loving father *and* mother present in their lives to grow up healthy and whole in mind, body, and soul. Without Ruth and Boaz, there is no David. Without a David, we never escape the social chaos, then or now.

The height of biblical love poetry is the Song of Songs, and while we can learn much from it, perhaps we can focus on the *beauty of chastity.* "A garden locked is my sister, my bride," Solomon says (Sg 4:12). Premarital chastity for bride and groom enables total self-gift. One can give to one's spouse a treasure never shared with another. That intimacy gives delight and strength to a marriage.

The Song also stresses the *holiness of the body.* The bride describes the bridegroom's body like the Temple; he describes her like the Garden of Eden, the first sanctuary. In the new covenant, St. Paul stresses, "Your body is a temple of the Holy Spirit" (1 Cor 6:19). This truth brings us back to chastity. Some think the Church and the Bible teach that the physical union of marriage is bad. On the contrary, they teach that the physical union of marriage is holy and therefore only to be celebrated by spouses. Just as Holy Orders ordains a man to handle the holy Body of Jesus in the Eucharist, so Matrimony "ordains" the spouses to handle the holy bodies of one another in a sacred way. For a seminarian to attempt to celebrate Mass the day before his ordination would be profane and a sacrilege. The day after his ordination, the exact same words and actions constitute the holiest act he could perform and, in fact, a sacred duty. For an engaged couple to join their bodies the day before their wedding would be profane and a sin, but the day after, it is the celebration of a holy sacrament and a sacred duty.

After the Song, some of the greatest love poetry in the Bible comes from the prophets, as they describe the romance of God with Israel. And from them we learn the principle of *indissolubility*. God never reneges on his covenant oaths, even when his bridal people go astray, as one of the earliest prophets tells us (Hos 1–3, esp. ch. 2). And the voice of the last prophet rings out emphatically, "'For I hate divorce! says the LORD God of Israel!'" (Mal 2:15–16).

God's commitment to that indissoluble covenant bond is perfectly expressed in Jesus Christ, who comes as a bridegroom to woo his people back to him. We see that story in every gospel but most strongly in the Gospel of John. From John we learn the role of matrimony as a *source of grace.* The great signs of abundance that Jesus performs in his ministry, such as creating hundreds of gallons of wine, and fish and chips for thousands, signify the abundance of grace present in each of the sacraments: "From his fulness have we all received, grace upon grace" (Jn 1:16). We usually talk about the infinite grace available from God in Baptism and the Eucharist, but we should include Matrimony there as well. When husband and wife embrace the role of being Jesus to each other, God unleashes a fountain of grace in the marriage that can lead both spouses to great holiness.

That's exactly Paul's vision of marriage in his famous teaching in Ephesians 5. St. Paul sees spouses as being Jesus to each other. There is so much to draw from his teaching, but perhaps we can focus on the role of *placing*

the other first. That involves "placing oneself under," as we discussed. Husbands "place themselves under" by laying down their lives, to death if necessary, for the well-being of their wives; wives "place themselves under" by showing their husbands respect for their role as head of the family, in imitation of Christ.

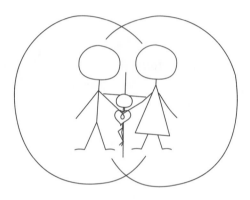

Finally, Revelation reminds us of the goal of all things, the purpose of human history and each of our own lives. And that is *happiness.* Not some cheap, self-centered, self-indulgent happiness of binge-watching shows or spending a week at an amusement park, but the deep, rich, and satisfying happiness of enjoying intimate communion with other persons. The closest natural experience we human beings have to the joy of heaven on this earth is in the marriage bond, so God uses wedding imagery to teach us what heaven will be like (Rv 21–22). We learn that *marriage is a foretaste of heaven.* Granted, marriage is also a serious matter, and some parts of this book have dealt with some serious themes, but Revelation reminds us that there *is* a happy ending! The story of salvation is actually a romantic comedy, a "rom-com," as we used to call them. Not in the sense that salvation history is cheap-date movie, but in the classic sense; the ancients called a story with a happy ending a comedy. The story of salvation is a romantic comedy because it is literally about love from beginning to end!

Notes

1. Thomas Aquinas, *Summa Theologica* I–II, Q.1, a.4, r.1.

2. See Edward P. Sri, "The Law of the Gift: Understanding the Two Sides of Love," *Lay Witness* (September/October 2005).

3. John Bergsma and Brant Pitre, *A Catholic Introduction to the Bible: Old Testament* (San Francisco: Ignatius, 2018), 182.

4. "Lovers" here refers to foreign gods and foreign kings. Israel allied herself to pagan nations and worshipped their gods.

5. The Pharisees were divided into two schools of thought following Rabbis Shammai (50 BC–AD 30) and Hillel (110 BC–AD 10), respectively. Shammai allowed a man to divorce only if his wife was unchaste; Hillel allowed him to divorce if she served him a bad meal. A third rabbi, Akiba (AD 50–135), permitted divorce even if a man just saw a prettier woman he wanted to marry (see m. *Gittin* 9:10, *The Mishnah*, trans. Herbert Danby [Oxford: Clarendon Press, 1933], 321). Opposed to the Pharisees were the sect of the Essenes, who promoted lifelong monogamy based on what they called "the

principle of creation" (Damascus Document [CD] 4:21). Since God made one man and one woman, and all the animals boarded the ark in pairs of male and female, the Essenes reasoned that God's plan was one man and one woman together for life. They permitted divorce in the sense of separation, but not remarriage (see Damascus Document [CD] 4:20–5:2; 11QTemple^a [11Q19] 57:17–19).

6. The NABRE correctly captures the meaning but not the wording. The Greek reads, "except for *porneia*," a word meaning "sexual immorality." Many Protestants have taken this to mean adultery and so allow for divorce if one's spouse has been unfaithful. However, there is a Greek word for adultery, *moicheia*, and Jesus doesn't use it here. The Greek *porneia* was commonly used to translate the Hebrew word *zĕnûth*, "sexual uncleanness," which covered any kind of improper intercourse, including people in an unlawful marriage because they were too closely related (see Leviticus 18:6–23). In the time of Jesus and the early church, the Gentiles permitted and practiced such marriages. For example, the royal family adopted Gentile customs, and Herod Antipas, ruler of Galilee, was himself in such a relationship with his brother's wife, Herodias. John the Baptist had insisted he end the marriage (Mt 14:1–4). In Matthew 19:9, Jesus qualifies that divorce is permissible in such a situation of an "unclean" (*porneia, zĕnûth*) union, since it is not a marriage in the eyes of God. See Joseph Fitzmyer, "The Matthean Divorce Texts and Some New Palestinian Evidence," *Theological Studies* 37 (1976): 197–226.

7. The NABRE captures the sense but does not translate literally. The Greek of Matthew 19:12 actually uses the word "eunuch," signifying a man who has been rendered incapable of fatherhood. The RSV reads more accurately:

"For there are eunuchs who have been so from birth, and there are eunuchs who have been made eunuchs by men, and there are eunuchs who have made themselves eunuchs for the sake of the kingdom of heaven." The "eunuchs who have made themselves eunuchs for the sake of the kingdom" are those who have committed themselves to a celibate life to prepare for the coming age of the Messiah. These would include John the Baptist, many in the Essene movement (like the "monks" at Qumrān), and Jesus himself. Jesus commends this as the best choice of lifestyle, provided God has enabled them (cf. 1 Cor 7:7).

8. Fr. Timothy Vaverek explains this wonderfully in *As I Have Loved You: Rediscovering Our Salvation in Christ* (Steubenville, OH: Emmaus Road, 2022).

9. See my *New Testament Basics for Catholics* (Notre Dame, IN: Ave Maria Press, 2015), 277–82.

John Bergsma is a professor of theology at the Franciscan University of Steubenville. He served as a Protestant pastor for four years before entering the Catholic Church in 2001 while pursuing a doctorate specializing in the Old Testament and the Dead Sea Scrolls from the University of Notre Dame.

In addition to teaching scripture at Franciscan, Bergsma is a frequent guest on Catholic radio, and he speaks regularly at conferences and parishes nationwide. Bergsma has published a number of academic and popular works on the Bible and the Catholic faith, including *Bible Basics for Catholics*, *New Testament Basics for Catholics*, *Psalm Basics for Catholics*, and *A Catholic Introduction to the Bible: Old Testament*.

He and his wife, Dawn, live with their children in Steubenville, Ohio.

ALSO BY
JOHN BERGSMA

Bible Basics for Catholics
A New Picture of Salvation History

John Bergsma's bestselling *Bible Basics for Catholics* offers readers
an accessible vision of salvation history as it unfolds in the Bible.
Readers will begin to see the Christian understanding of salvation by
walking through the Old Testament, going through the great stories
of Adam and Eve, Noah, Abraham, Moses, the great kings and prophets
of Israel, and culminating in the person and work of Jesus Christ.

ALSO AVAILABLE IN SPANISH!

New Testament Basics for Catholics

In *New Testament Basics for Catholics,* John Bergsma
uses simple illustrations and a clear, conversational style
to introduce four of the most important writers
in the New Testament: Matthew, Luke, Paul, and John.

Psalm Basics for Catholics
Seeing Salvation History in a New Way

In *Psalm Basics for Catholics,* John Bergsma highlights the presence
of Jesus in the psalms and helps us understand their meaning
in light of the story of salvation to bridge the gap between the world
of contemporary Catholics and the ancient world of the Bible.